the Precision system
of contract bridge
bidding

Chas. H. Goren

presents

the Precision system
of contract bridge
bidding

by Charles H. Goren

edited by Robert B. Ewen

A CHANCELLOR HALL *book*

published by DOUBLEDAY & COMPANY, INC.

Garden City, New York

Library of Congress Catalogue No.: 74–155061

Designed and produced by Chancellor Hall, Ltd.
Printed in the United States of America

Contents

Foreword

FOR NEARLY TWO GENERATIONS, the vast majority of players have described their method of playing bridge as "the Goren System." I have given up on convincing them that a Goren System has never existed. Rather, what they play is the Goren method, based on the point count I introduced, enabling bridge players to evaluate the worth of both the high cards and the distributional power of their hands, and to express this valuation accurately and simply.

I think I may take credit for eliminating some of the 800-point sets resulting from such auctions as:

1 NT	PASS	2 NT	PASS
3 NT	PASS	PASS	DBL.
PASS	PASS	PASS	

I believe I helped players to recognize that they needed a combined 26 points for game at notrump or a major suit. I helped them to determine when their combined assets would justify a slam, a game or only a part score. Poor players lost less; good players won more; most players argued more briefly if not less often. If a difference of opinion arose, my book,* if one happened to be handy, helped to resolve the case. But I did not invent contract bridge, or change its laws, or claim to have created such innovations as the Blackwood Convention to find out about aces and kings or the two club response to a one notrump opening, aimed at locating a possible fit in a four-card major suit. If something good fitted into "Standard American" bidding, I endorsed and explained it. I avoided incorporating gadgets that merely complicate the game, and so the vast majority play "according to Goren," and Americans on the whole play very good bridge.

Came the Italians

Then there began a phenomenon it is impossible to ignore. For a dozen years, Italian teams won the world championships. This could be explained by the fact that they were wonderful players, but it was also true that they all used as their forcing opening an artificial bid of one club. They didn't invent the principle—in fact, it was first introduced by the American who invented contract bridge, Harold S. Vanderbilt. Furthermore, they did not agree among themselves on what the one club bid should mean; the most recent line-ups of the vaunted Blue Team have used no fewer than three different systems. True, the one club opening came along more often than the powerhouse two bid or the artificial two-club bid used by the rest of the world, but the Italian successes were long attributed to the merits of their players rather than of their systems.

However, in 1969 and again in 1970, two "miracles" occurred in World Championship competition. In each case a lightly held group of players, boasting virtually no world-class experience and obviously lacking in the technical playing skills of many of their rivals, carried teams representing Nationalist China into the Bermuda Bowl finals and gave them the runner-up spot playing against some of the world's best trained and most talented players. They too were employing a one-club convention, but their Precision Club bid seemed to occur almost twice as frequently. The reason was the seemingly minute one point lower minimum requirement for the club opening—a reduction to 16 points from the 17 used by the Italians and others.

Like my own distributional point count, the Precision method is the brainchild of an engineer, who adapted thinking to the performance of what will nevertheless continue to be considered an art—the art of successful bidding.

C. C. Wei, the creator of Precision, was born in China but has long been a citizen of the United States. He is a builder and operator of tanker ships and what he has accomplished in that field is perhaps even more remarkable than the contribution he has made to contract bridge. Wei's primary aim, like my own, is not just to create champions—although he has succeeded far beyond his own expectations in accomplishing this—but to make better bridge easier and more fun for the average players.

No, I am not changing the "Goren System." You do not need to play an artificial one club forcing bid in order to enjoy bridge. But if you have become impressed with the virtues of an opening one club bid as the cornerstone of a system, the one that I recommend you learn is C. C. Wei's "Precision" method, as explained here. Aside from the merits that you will be able to judge for yourself, you cannot fail to be impressed by the fact that the system, plus Wei's training method, helped five relatively unknown players to win the American Contract Bridge League's National Knockout Team championship in 1970. In addition it has brought numerous other successes to lesser lights. Also by the fact that it has been adopted for trial by such American greats as Robert Jordan and Arthur Robinson, Alvin Roth, and many other stars yet to be announced. And by two members of the former Blue Team: Benito Garozzo and Giorgio Belladonna!

I would like to thank these and the many other expert players who have assisted me in the analysis and exposition of the Precision System as presented here. I would especially like to thank Dr. Robert Ewen, associate professor of psychology at New York University, the major editor of this book and the author of a magnificent book on Opening Leads. I am happy to welcome him as a member of the Goren Editorial Board.

Charles H. Goren.

tho Precision system
of contract bridge
bidding

1

Why Precision works

SOME TIME AGO, I chanced upon a bridge acquaintance of mine who blithely informed me that he was giving up Goren. "The trouble with my game is that I've been using the wrong bidding system," he announced confidently. "I'm going to switch to expert methods so I can win more often!" Struggling under the load of an immense pile of bridge books, he headed off to do some concentrated studying.

In the following months, my friend tried a vast number of systems. Unfortunately, the only noticeable result was a substantial increase in the number of horrendous catastrophes and unbelievable disasters that he produced, but somehow this seemed to make him even more determined. When he informed me, with a fiendish gleam in his eye, that his latest plan was to devise a radical new system of his own which combined the most complicated features of Marmic (in which a pass in first or second position shows 16–19 points) and the original Little Major (in which an opening bid of 1 ♡ or 1 ♠ shows 5–9 points and no more than three cards in the suit bid), I decided that it was high time to have a word with him. My advice fell upon deaf ears, however, and it was not until his new system resulted in a two-diamond contract on a hand which was cold for a grand slam in either major suit or notrump and a 3400 point set in the same evening that he finally decided that standard Goren was not so bad after all.

My friend's troubles came about because he failed to realize two important facts about bidding systems. First, systems that work well when used by famous experts are *not* necessarily good prescriptions for the majority of bridge players. An expert may win with a system that is undistinguished or one that is full of frightening complexities—after all, he is an expert! Second, some systems contain major theoretical flaws. That is, they introduce a few bidding gadgets that are effective for certain kinds of hands, at the cost of making other bids do so much extra duty that some common hands become completely unbiddable. As a result, any gains produced by the gadgets are likely to be more than offset by losses that arise from the system's "weak spots."

In contrast to this gloomy picture, one recently developed system has achieved remarkable success. Using the Precision system, a relatively inexperienced Chinese team defeated far more practiced opponents to finish second in both the 1969 and 1970 World Championships; and a team of young, lesser-known players bested the cream of America's bridge experts to win the 1970 U.S. Summer National Spingold Team Championship. These impressive results make clear that here, for once, is an effective system. Why has Precision succeeded where so many others have failed?

The advantage of limited bids

Suppose your partner opens the bidding with 1 NT, showing 16–18 points and balanced suit distribution (4-3-3-3, 4-4-3-2, or 5-3-3-2 where the five-card suit is a minor). You hold:

♠ A 6 3
♡ K 8 2
◊ 9 4
♣ K 10 9 7 3

"Aha," I can hear you thinking, "this is an easy one. I have 10 high-card points and partner has 16–18, so the combined partnership total is 26–28 points. We therefore must have the 26 points needed to justify a game bid and are far from the 33 points required for a small slam. Since partner's hand and my hand are both balanced, I'll simply raise to 3 NT." You know, of course, that there is no guarantee that three notrump will make; but you can tell—after just one bid from partner!—that three notrump is overwhelmingly likely to be the best contract.

The real hero of this successful auction is the opening bid of 1 NT. This bid is *limited;* that is, it defines partner's hand within a narrow range of point values and distributions. Since it gives you such a clear picture of partner's holding, it is the work of but a moment for you to select the proper contract.

Now suppose instead that your partner opens the bidding with 1 ♡. This time, you will have more work to do before you can decide on the probable best contract! If partner has a balanced minimum such as

> ♠ Q J 7
> ♡ A 10 4 3
> ◊ A Q 10 2
> ♣ 6 4

you should settle for a part score, preferably in notrump. If partner has some extra values and a five-card or longer heart suit, such as

> ♠ K Q 2
> ♡ A Q J 6 4
> ◊ J 5 3
> ♣ A 6

four hearts will be the winning contract; while if partner should happen to hold

> ♠ 7
> ♡ A 7 5 4
> ◊ A K 5 3
> ♣ A Q J 8

the proper contract is six clubs!* Contracts such as heart and club partials and three notrump are also distinct possibilities. With so many alternatives to contend with, it will take far more than just one bid from partner before you can tell what the final contract should be.

The culprit that is making you work so hard in this in-

---

* Declarer can count five club tricks, two diamond tricks, two heart tricks, and a spade trick on top, and readily negotiates the two additional tricks that he needs by simply ruffing two low spades before drawing all the trumps.

stance is the *unlimited* opening bid of 1 ♡. For this bid, partner can have from 13 to 22+ points and from four to seven or eight hearts, and these ranges are so wide that you must obtain considerably more information about partner's hand before you can determine the best contract.

Thus, bidding will be easier, and your results more accurate, whenever you or your partner can correctly make a limited bid. Note that this applies not just to the opening bid, but to all subsequent bidding as well. For example, if you open 1 ♡ and partner makes the limited response of 1 NT (6–9 points, balanced suit distribution), often you can decide immediately upon the best contract. If, however, he makes an unlimited response such as 1 ♠ (6–17 points, four or more spades), you will need more information, because relatively little is known about his point count and distribution.

One of the ways in which the Precision system strives for greater bidding accuracy is by increasing the number of limited bids. For example, the opening bids of 1 ♣, 1 ♢, 1 ♡, and 1 ♠ are all *relatively unlimited* (13 to 22+ points) in standard Goren. In Precision, however, all but one of these very common opening bids are *limited*. This startling change is accomplished by the judicious use of appropriate conventional bids.

Conventional bids

Every bid conveys a message. For example, a Goren 1 ♡ opening bid announces possession of at least 13 points and at least four hearts. It is a *natural* bid—it promises strength in the suit actually named, hearts. Under the laws of bridge, however, it is quite permissible to use what are called *conventional* bids, which convey messages that have no relationship whatsoever to the denomination (suit or notrump) named in the bid.* For example, you and your partner may, if you wish, agree to use

---

* Weird conventions designed solely to confuse and intimidate the opponents, however, are barred from tournament play (and are also a poor idea in home games for those who have any hope of playing sociably against the same opponents in the future).

a 2 ♣ response to an opening bid of 1 NT to ask opener to bid a four-card major suit if he has one and to bid 2 ◊ otherwise (the "Stayman convention"). This 2 ♣ response is conventional because it does not promise possession of a club suit and does not express any interest in making clubs the final contract; in fact, it has nothing at all to do with clubs. Another well-known example is the Blackwood 4 NT convention, in which a 4 NT bid asks partner how many aces he holds and has nothing to do with notrump.

Obviously, conventions must be designed with care. It would be suicidal to use an opening bid of 7 ◊ to convey the message "I have a ghastly hand!" for you would ultimately be required to play at the seven-level with your ghastly hand, much to your opponents' glee (and profit). On the other hand, a convention that looks odd at first glance may actually have considerable merit. For example, suppose that the following conventional meaning is assigned to an opening bid of 1 ♣: "Partner, I have a hand with 16 or more points. I might have any distribution — even a void in clubs." Clearly, some details will have to be worked out before this 1 ♣ convention can be put into practice. We will have to require that partner respond even with zero points, so as to avoid the ignominy of being passed in 1 ♣ with a club void and a strong two-bid on the side; methods will be needed to avoid trouble when partner makes a forced response with a bust; opener will need a bid for a hand such as

♠ A 8 5
♡ 7
◊ 9 7 6
♣ A K J 7 4 3

now that a 1 ♣ opening is reserved solely to announce a hand of 16 points or more. The 1 ♣ convention offers a major compensating advantage, however: Since hands with 16 or more points are opened 1 ♣, *all other opening bids* are limited to 15 points or less.* For this reason, the 1 ♣ convention is one of the cornerstones of the Precision system.

* Except the 2 NT opening bid, which retains its usual meaning.

As an illustration, consider the hand discussed earlier:

♠ A 6 3
♡ K 8 2
◊ 9 4
♣ K 10 9 7 3

Suppose now that you and your partner are playing Precision, and he opens the bidding with 1 ♡. You know that he has a maximum of 15 points because he did not open 1 ♣. Also, as we will see later, the distribution of the Precision 1 ♡ opening is also limited; this bid promises at least *five* hearts. Therefore, you can immediately draw the following deductions:

1] Since a combined total of at least *eight* cards in a suit will ensure a playable trump suit, and since partner has at least five hearts and you have three, hearts will be a satisfactory trump suit.

2] Slam is out of the question.

3] Game should be bid if opener has a maximum hand (15 points or a good 14).

Therefore, you would simply choose the appropriate Precision bid that invites game in hearts and leave the rest up to your partner. As you can see, the limited nature of the 1 ♡ opening bid, made possible by the conventional meaning assigned to the 1 ♣ opening, greatly simplifies this auction.

Why Precision works

Precision is not the only system which uses a conventional 1 ♣ opening bid. However, some of the other one-club systems involve so many abstruse conventions and complexities that they are beyond the grasp of all but the most dedicated expert. Still other one-club systems sacrifice accuracy for simplicity and consequently contain some grievous theoretical flaws; for example, one such system necessitates a (non-conventional!) 1 ◊ opening bid on certain hands with a singleton or doubleton diamond.

Such serious weaknesses are likely to cost the user far more than the conventional bids gain.

Precision, however, is a primarily natural system which contains a relatively small number of conventions, so you do not need to be a memory expert or a world champion to learn it. In addition, each convention was added to the system only after it met two critical requirements: *1]* The convention was deemed necessary to satisfy a vital function (such as increasing the number of limited opening bids), and *2]* it was ascertained that no major weaknesses would spring up elsewhere in the system as a result of the convention. Thus, you can enjoy the benefits of the convention—namely, avoiding the ambiguities that plague other systems and finding out what you need to know in order to reach the best contract—without paying the price of having a serious weakness elsewhere in the system to worry about. Of course, basic Precision cannot handle every conceivable situation; no system can do that. It *is* designed to deal effectively with the great majority of situations that you are likely to encounter at the bridge table.

A brief outline of Precision

The Precision system will be presented in detail in subsequent chapters of this book. Before making a close inspection of the trees, however, it is an excellent idea to understand the general nature of the forest, so let's begin with a consideration of the overall structure of Precision.

Counting points

In Precision, high-card points are counted in the usual way:

$$
\begin{aligned}
\text{Ace} &= 4 \\
\text{King} &= 3 \\
\text{Queen} &= 2 \\
\text{Jack} &= 1
\end{aligned}
$$

Distribution points, however, are counted *only when raising partner's suit.* They are evaluated as follows:

$$\text{Void} = 5$$
$$\text{Singleton} = 3$$
$$\text{Doubleton} = 1$$

Distribution points are *not* counted when you are planning to play in notrump, even if you have raised partner's suit somewhere along the way. In a suit contract, shortness in your side suits allows you to ruff in quickly and prevent the opponents from running an unpleasantly large number of tricks; but you can't trump anything in a notrump contract. Also, if you don't have many trumps to ruff with, your suit contract may turn into a "notrump" contract even though you didn't plan it that way. Therefore, distribution points are counted only when you intend to play in a suit contract and your side has an ample supply of trumps (usually at least *eight* in the combined hands) and this will usually be true when you raise your partner's suit

Certain high-card point totals represent particularly important milestones:

8 points: Minimum for opening weak two-bid,
        or one-level forcing response to limited opening,
        or positive response to 1 ♣ opening,
        or single raise of opener's major

11 points: Minimum for limited opening bid,
        or two-over-one forcing response to limited opening,
        or double raise of opener's major

16 points: Minimum for 1 ♣ opening bid,
        or game-forcing response to limited opening

22 points: Minimum for 2 NT opening bid,
        or jump rebid after 1 ♣ opening and 1 ◇ response

In Precision, a combined total of *25 points* is sufficient to justify a game declaration. (This differs from the Goren 26-point total partly because opener does not count distribution points, and partly because an exhaustive analysis of world championship hands has shown that game was made with this total half of the time.)

To illustrate the counting of points, suppose you are the dealer and hold our by now familiar example hand:

♠ A 6 3
♡ K 8 2
◊ 9 4
♣ K 10 9 7 3

You cannot possibly raise partner's suit since he hasn't bid anything yet, so do *not* count any distribution points for the doubleton diamond; your hand is worth 10 points. Let us suppose that you elect to pass. If partner opens 1 ♡, promising at least five hearts and a maximum of 15 points,* you will raise hearts and therefore you *do* count one point for the doubleton diamond, making your hand worth 11 points. If, however, partner opens 1 ◊ (which shows a maximum of 15 points and at least four diamonds), you certainly do not intend to raise on your doubleton, so the value of your hand remains at 10 points.

As a second example, suppose you hold

♠ A Q J 8 3
♡ A 8 6 4
◊ K 6 3 2
♣ ———

This hand is worth 14 points for purposes of opening the bidding, as you do not count any points for the club void at this stage. If, however, you open 1 ♠ and partner responds 2 ♡, you will be delighted to raise with your fine support and even more delighted to watch the value of your hand zoom to 19 points, counting 5 points for the void in clubs.

---

* When you encounter terms such as "15 points" in this book, remember that only *high-card* points are included in the total for a hand *unless* the bidder plans to raise partner's suit, in which case distribution points are also counted. Thus, in this instance, distribution points cannot possibly be included in the total as opener is *not* raising a suit bid by his partner.

PRECISION SYSTEM

TABLE 1.
An Outline of Precision Opening Bids and First Responses

OPENING BID	FIRST RESPONSES
Only high-card points are counted when opening the bidding.	Only high-card points are counted unless responder is raising (or plans to raise) opener's suit.
1 ♣: *Conventional.* Shows **16 or more points.**	**1 ◇:** *Conventional.* Shows 0-7 points. **1 ♡, 1 ♠, 2 ♣, 2 ◇:** Natural, 8 or more points; at least 5 cards in bid suit. **1 NT, 2 NT, 3 NT:** Natural, limited. *Suit jumps:* Natural weak preempts.
1 ◇: 11-15 points, usually at least four diamonds.	**1 ♡, 1 ♠, 2 ♣:** Natural, one-round force. **1 NT, 3 NT:** Natural, limited. **2 NT:** Natural, 16 or more points and a balanced hand. Game force. **2 ◇:** Strong diamond raise. One-round force. **3 ◇:** Weak diamond raise. **2 ♡, 2 ♠, 3 ♣:** Natural, 16 or more points with strong 5-card or longer suit; game force.
1 ♡, 1 ♠: 11-15 points, at least five cards in bid suit.	*New suit:* Natural, one-round force. *Raises:* Natural, limited. **1 NT:** One-round force. **2 NT:** Natural, 16 or more points and a balanced hand. Game force. **3 NT:** *Conventional.* Strong raise; limited. *New suit jumps:* Natural, 16 or more points with strong 5-card or longer suit; game force.
1 NT: 13-15 points, balanced suit distribution.	**2 ♣:** Non-forcing Stayman. **2 ◇:** Forcing Stayman. **2 ♡, 2 ♠, 3 ♣, 3 ◇:** Signoff. **2 NT:** Natural, invitational (10-11 points). **3 NT:** Signoff (12-15 points). **3 ♡, 3 ♠:** Natural, forcing.
2 ♣: 11-15 points, at least five good clubs with a four-card major suit *or* six good clubs. **2 ◇:** *Conventional.* 4-4-1-4 or 4-4-0-5 distribution with short *diamonds;* **11-15 points.**	**2 ◇:** *Conventional.* Requests more information **2 ♡, 2 ♠, 3 ♣:** Natural. **2 NT:** Natural, limited. *Any game bid:* Signoff. **2 ♡, 2 ♠, 3 ♣:** Signoff. **2 NT:** *Conventional.* Requests more information **3 ◇:** Natural, invitational to **3 NT.** *Any game bid:* Signoff.
2 ♡, 2 ♠: Weak two-bids.	*New suit:* Natural, forcing. **2 NT:** *Conventional.* Requests more information *Any game bid:* Signoff.
2 NT: **22-23 points,** balanced suit distribution.	"Standard" responses.
3 or 4 of suit: Preemptive.	"Standard" responses.

The general structure of opening bids and responses

The overall structure of Precision opening bids and responses is summarized in Table 1 for ready reference. Let's take a closer look at some of the entries in the table and see how the various parts of the system combine to produce a meaningful whole.

Opening bids with strong hands.

All hands with 16 or more points are opened either with 1 ♣ or 2 NT. Consequently, all other opening bids deny as many as 16 points. The 1 ♣ opener clarifies the nature of his hand (which may be anything from a balanced 16-count to a strong two-bid) by means of his subsequent rebids.

Opening bids with balanced minimums.

Hands with balanced suit distribution (4-3-3-3, 4-4-3-2, or 5-3-3-2 where the five-card suit is a minor) and 13–15 points are opened with 1 NT. With balanced hands worth 12 points or less, it is usually wisest to let discretion be the better part of valor and pass.

Some examples:

♠ A Q 8 6　♡ A J 3　◊ 6 4 2　♣ Q 9 8:
　Open 1 NT.

♠ 7 3　♡ A K 8 7　◊ K Q 4 2　♣ K 10 4:
　Open 1 NT.

♠ Q 8 6　♡ 10 4　◊ A K 10　♣ A J 4 3 2:
　Open 1 NT.

♠ K J 8　♡ Q 10 4　◊ J 4 3　♣ A J 4 2:
　Pass.

Opening bids with unbalanced minimums.

Unbalanced hands with 11–15 points and a suit containing *five* or more cards are usually opened by bidding the longest suit. In case of ties, the *higher-ranking* suit is selected. However, since 1 ♣ openings are reserved for hands with 16 or more points, hands with club suits must be opened with 2 ♣. Beginning the auction at the *two-level* is somewhat risky, so it is better to seek an alternative unless your club suit is strong.

Some examples:

♠ 8 6 3   ♡ K 10 7 4   ◊ A K J 8 6   ♣ 8:
    Open 1 ◊.

♠ 7 3   ♡ A Q 8 6 4   ◊ K J 3   ♣ A 4 3:
    Open 1 ♡.

♠ 6 2   ♡ Q 10 9 4 3   ◊ 7   ♣ A K Q J 4:
    Open 1 ♡.

♠ 10 8 7 4 2   ♡ A J 7 4   ◊ A K 2   ♣ 3:
    Open 1 ♠.

♠ A 8 5   ♡ 7   ◊ 9 7 6   ♣ A K J 7 4 3:
    Open 2 ♣.

♠ 6   ♡ A J 7 5 4   ◊ 8   ♣ A Q 10 8 4 2:
    Open 2 ♣.

♠ Q 6 3   ♡ 7 4   ◊ A 8 2   ♣ A J 4 3 2:
    Pass. (The clubs are too weak to open 2 ♣.)

The only unbalanced distribution which lacks a five-card suit is 4-4-4-1. With a 4-4-4-1 hand which includes four diamonds, such as

♠ A Q 7 6
♡ K 9 7 4
◊ A J 6 3
♣ 7

open 1 ◊. (A 1 ♠ or 1 ♡ opening would promise a five-card or longer suit.) This is the only natural suit opening bid that can be made with as few as four cards in the bid suit. You should also open 1 ◊ with

♠ 4
♡ A K 3
◊ A J 10 5
♣ Q 7 6 4 3

rather than bid the anemic club suit at the two-level or bid notrump with unbalanced suit distribution.

There is one distributional minimum that is not provided for by any of the above opening bids—a 4-4-1-4 hand with a singleton diamond. Suppose you hold

♠ A Q 7 6
♡ K 9 7 4
◊ 7
♣ A J 6 3

You have 14 points and should certainly open the bidding. But with what? You can't open 1 NT with an unbalanced hand; you can't open 1 ♡ or 1 ♠ lacking a five-card suit; you can't open 1 ♣ with less than 16 points; and you certainly don't dare open 2 ♣ with a four-card suit or 1 ◊ with a singleton diamond. A 4-4-0-5 hand with a void in diamonds and a weak five-card club suit creates similar problems. Therefore, a special opening bid is needed for such hands, and an opening 2 ◊ bid is assigned the conventional meaning of 11–15 points and 4-4-1-4 distribution, or 4-4-0-5 distribution including five *clubs*, with *shortness in diamonds*. Since partner knows your hand within very narrow limits and has three good choices for a trump suit if he wishes to end the auction quickly before something disastrous happens, the risk inherent in this highly informative two-level opening bid is not great.

Preemptive openings.

Since all strong hands are opened with 1 ♣, opening bids of 2 ♡ and 2 ♠ are used as weak two-bids. These bids are preemptive and show a good six-card holding in the suit bid with little of value on the side.

For example:

♠ A Q J 8 6 3   ♡ Q 3 2   ◇ 8 6 3   ♣ 10:
Open 2 ♠.

♠ 7   ♡ Q 8 6 4 3 2   ◇ 9 6 3   ♣ Q 4 2:
Pass. (The hearts are too weak.)

♠ 9   ♡ K Q 10 5 4 3   ◇ A 4 3   ♣ Q 10 5:
Open 1 ♡.
> (Too much side strength for a weak two-bid.)

Opening bids of three and four of a suit retain the standard preemptive meaning.

These opening bids will be discussed in more detail in subsequent chapters. Let us now briefly consider the structure of the first response.

Responses to 1 ♣.
Responder *must* bid; opener could have game in his own hand! A 1 ◇ response is conventional and shows 0–7 points; this prevents matters from getting out of hand when responder has a bust. Thus, the opening 1 ♣ bid says "I have a good hand" and the 1 ◇ response says "*I* don't!" Other responses are natural. Notrump and non-jump suit responses promise at least 8 points and usually lead to game.

Responses to 1 ◇, 1 ♡, and 1 ♠.
An outline of the responses to opening bids of 1 ◇, 1 ♡, and 1 ♠ is included in the table for your convenience, but there is no need to dwell on them at this point. Since these opening bids are both natural and limited, the response structure is straightforward; you can probably even use your current methods intact with fair success. As we will see, however, it is possible to take advantage of the precise nature of these opening bids to further facilitate the subsequent auction; for example, responder should pass with 6 or 7 points and a tolerance for

opener's suit because opener is known to hold a maximum of 15 points.

Responses to 1 NT.

As is indicated in the table, responses to an opening bid of 1 NT are relatively standard, but take into account opener's below-standard range of 13–15 points.

Responses to 2 ♣.

Responder passes with club tolerance and no chance for game opposite a 14 or 15 point maximum. Responses of 2 ♡, 2 ♠, and 2 NT are natural and fairly weak, although game may still be reached; a 3 ♣ raise is natural and invitational. The 2 ♢ response is conventional and requests more information about opener's hand, and is most helpful to responder for purposes of investigating a possible slam or notrump game. Any jump to game is a signoff.

Responses to 2 ♢.

Since opener has at most one diamond, responder should pass only with six or more diamonds and no prospects of game. Any non-jump new suit bid is a signoff, indicating that responder sees no hope for game and wants to end the auction as soon as possible. The 2 NT response is conventional and requests more information about opener's hand. Any jump to game is a signoff.

Responses to 2 ♡ and 2 ♠.

If you are familiar with weak two-bids, you can use your usual responses; if not, the responses recommended by Precision will be discussed in a subsequent chapter.

Responses to 2 NT and 3 or 4 of a suit.

These responses are relatively standard and hence need not be taken up at this point.

The Precision system is presented in detail in the following chapters. Don't try to master it all in one evening; learning any new system requires care and effort. You should find, however, that Precision is enjoyable, logical, and not hard to learn.* There are quizzes at the end of each chapter that you can use to check your progress until you are ready to take the final "test" at the bridge table. Good luck!

---

* C. C. Wei has developed valuable methods for obtaining partnership practice before venturing into actual play:

1] To practice auctions beginning with 1 ♣, remove three small cards in each suit from the deck and deal 13 cards to each partner.

2] To practice major-suit opening bids, remove three small cards in each *minor* suit from the deck and deal 13 cards to each partner.

3] To practice auctions beginning with 1 ◊ or 2 ♣ opening bids, remove three small cards in each *major* suit before dealing the customary 13 cards to each partner.

4] To practice auctions beginning with an opening bid of 2 ◊, remove all diamonds *except* the ace, four, three, and two from the deck before dealing.

2

The forcing 1♣ opening bid
and the first response

THE NEXT SEVERAL CHAPTERS will deal with those happy occasions when your side is able to open the bidding with 1 ♣, announcing possession of a strong hand and instilling fear and trembling in the hearts of the opponents.

The forcing 1♣ opening bid

With one exception, *all* hands with 16 or more points are opened with 1 ♣. The exception occurs in the case of hands with balanced suit distribution and 22–23 points, which are opened with 2 NT. Remember that in Precision, only high-card points are counted unless you are raising partner's suit. Some examples:

♠ A K Q 8 7 4   ♡ A K 3 2   ◇ A 7 3   ♣ ——:
    Open 1 ♣.

♠ A 3   ♡ A J 8 7 5   ◇ K Q J 4   ♣ Q 3:
    Open 1 ♣.

♠ K Q 10   ♡ A J 3   ◇ A 10 4 3   ♣ Q 7 3:
    Open 1 ♣.

♠ Q J 7   ♡ A K J 8   ◇ A K Q 4   ♣ K 4:
    Open 2 NT.

♠ 8 7 3   ♡ A   ◇ K 8 3 2   ♣ A Q J 10 4:
    Do *not* open 1 ♣; you have only 14 points (Open 2 ♣.)

It would obviously be catastrophic to be passed out in 1 ♣ (particularly with the first example hand shown above!), but you need not worry about this dire occurrence. The 1 ♣ opening bid is *forcing,* and partner is expected to respond even with zero points.

Unusual cases

Strong two-suited hands.

Except for the possibility of decks prearranged by clever friends, the odds are overwhelmingly prohibitive against you or me ever holding

♠ A K Q J 10 9 8 7 6 5 4 3 2   ♡ ——   ◇ ——   ♣ ——

If such a miracle were to occur, however, you would surely not regard your hand as weak because you have only 10 high-card points! Nor should you, since point count is least accurate for wildly distributional hands.

Similar reasoning applies in the case of strong two-suited hands, which you *are* resonably likely to hold. For example, suppose you deal yourself

♠ 3
♡ A K Q 10 4
◇ A Q 9 6 3
♣ 7 2

This hand has exceptional trick-taking power; you need very little in partner's hand to have a reasonable play for game (four small hearts and the king of diamonds is enough). Therefore, you should open with 1 ♣ even though you have only 15 points. However, do *not* open 1 ♣ with

♠ A
♡ J 7 6 3 2
◇ A 9 6 4 3
♣ A Q

Although you have exactly the same point count and distribution as in the previous example,* too many of your high cards are outside your long suits for you to be highly enthusiastic about your prospects. That heart suit certainly won't take many tricks unless partner has quite a bit by way of support! Just open 1 ♡, showing 11–15 points and a five-card heart suit.

With longer suits, you can shade the point-count requirements for the 1 ♣ opening a bit more. The following 14-point hand is definitely worth an opening bid of 1 ♣:

> ♠ A K J 8 6 5
> ♡ 7
> ◊ A Q 10 4 3
> ♣ 6

Hands with negative features.

Hands with values largely consisting of queens and jacks, and hands which contain unprotected honors, may deceive the unwary bidder into thinking that he has more strength than is actually the case. For example, suppose you hold

> ♠ A Q J
> ♡ Q J 3 2
> ◊ Q J 6 3
> ♣ Q J

This hand counts to 16 points, but you will do well to take a second look before deciding upon your opening bid! You have a severe shortage of aces and kings, some of which will undoubtedly be unkind enough to reside with the opponents. To make matters worse, the unprotected club honors will produce absolutely no tricks at all if the oponents can cash the ace and king (although they *might* help set up a club suit in partner's hand such as ♣ 10 9 3 2). You should therefore conclude that this hand is definitely not as good as it might appear to be and

---

* You may have wondered whether the Precision practice of not counting distribution points when opening the bidding was responsible for the under-evaluation of the first example hand. This second example should make clear that this is *not* the case.

quietly open with 1 NT, showing 13–15 points and balanced suit distribution.

Notice that these unusual cases arise from problems in evaluating the strength of a hand, and are *not* caused by the Precision system. For example, aces (and also kings to some extent) are actually worth slightly more than the allotted high-card points, and unprotected honors are worth somewhat less than protected honors. Since no one wants to grapple with point-count methods that yield bizarre totals such as 16½ or 13⅞, some inaccuracies are inevitable. No method of hand evaluation has ever succeeded in making good judgment unnecessary, and none ever will—which helps make bridge the great game that it is.

The first response with weak hands
(0–7 points)

It is now time to move to the other side of the table and consider the first response to the 1 ♣ opening bid. The most obvious rule is that you should *never pass;* partner may not have any clubs at all, and will in any case be highly irritated at having to play the hand in a ridiculous contract if the 1 ♣ bid is passed out. Thus, the 1 ♣ opening bid is forcing; even with zero points, you *must* respond. To avoid reaching too high a contract when you have a bad hand and partner has a minimum, certain responses serve as warning flags which signal partner to proceed with caution.

Constructive responses
Responses of 2 ♡ and 2 ♠.

It would be a poor idea to use a jump in a major suit in response to partner's 1 ♣ opening to show a strong hand. If you have a powerful hand and he has enough strength to open 1 ♣, slam is a distinct possibility and you should leave yourself as much bidding room as possible for purposes of investigation. One of the more embarrassing blunders that a bridge player can commit is to go down one trick in a slam-investigating contract of 5 ♡ or 5 ♠, thereby losing out on the lucrative game bonus that would have been gained had the auction stopped at the four-level. Missing a cold slam because of fear of investigating past the game level is also not a great achievement. Therefore, as we will see shortly, simple (i.e., non-jump) suit responses are used with strong hands.

In Precision, the *constructive responses* of 2 ♡ and 2 ♠ show hands containing a six-card major suit and 4–7 points, most of which are in the bid suit (thus, a "mini" weak two-bid). For example, if partner opens 1 ♣, respond 2 ♡ with

> ♠ 8 7
> ♡ K J 10 6 5 2
> ◊ 7 5 3
> ♣ 9 4

or 2 ♠ with

> ♠ A Q J 8 6 3
> ♡ 7 4 2
> ◊ 6 5 3
> ♣ 4

This highly limited bid will make it easy for partner to select the best contract.

A two-level constructive response may also be made on a weak seven-card major suit headed by the jack. However, do *not* respond 2 ♡ or 2 ♠ with hands such as the following:

> ♠ J 8 6 4 3 2   ♡ 7   ◊ A J 6   ♣ 6 4 3
> (The spades are too weak.)

> ♠ A Q 8 4 3 2   ♡ Q 6 3   ◊ 5 4   ♣ 7 2
> (You have 8 points.)

> ♠ 7   ♡ Q 10 9 6 5 4   ◊ 8 4 3   ♣ 7 3 2
> (You have only 2 points.)

> ♠ 5 4   ♡ K Q 10 8 3   ◊ 10 5 4 2   ♣ 9 6
> (You have only a five-card heart suit.)

The last three examples are included to stress an important point: It is usually a poor idea to "cheat" on your point count or distribution. Limited bids are advantageous because they convey specific information; if you change the code without telling partner or expand the message to include too wide a range of hands, the ones most likely to gain an advantage are the opponents.

Responses of three of a suit.

A constructive response of three of a suit (including 3 ♣) to a 1 ♣ opening bid shows a *seven*-card suit and 4–7 points, most of which are in the bid suit (thus, a "mini" preempt). A three-level constructive response can also be made on a weak eight-card suit headed by the jack.

Some examples:

♠ J 8   ♡ 7 5   ◇ 6 5   ♣ A Q 10 8 7 5 2:
    Respond 3 ♣.

♠ 6   ♡ 7 2   ◇ A 9 8 6 5 4 3   ♣ 6 4 2:
    Respond 3 ◇.

♠ 10 3   ♡ K Q 10 9 7 4 3   ◇ 7 4 3   ♣ J:
    Respond 3 ♡.

♠ Q J 9 8 4 3 2   ♡ Q 5   ◇ J 6   ♣ 10 7:
    Respond 3 ♠.

As you can see, these responses are similar to the responses of 2 ♡ and 2 ♠ except that they show a seven-card suit. However, this is an important difference! The extra card in your long and fairly strong suit is worth one full trick and one fewer loser elsewhere, so your response of *three* of a suit may well provide the vital information that will enable partner to contract for a makable game or slam.

As the first example above shows, distribution points are *not* counted when responding to 1 ♣ even if you bid clubs. The

1 ♣ opening is conventional, so there is no possibility of raising partner's suit at this point; you don't yet know what his suit is —or even if he has one.

The negative 1 ◊ response

With any hand worth 7 points or less which does not qualify for a constructive response, your first obligation is to warn partner that you have only 0–7 points and that game is therefore unlikely unless he has substantial extra values. Saying "I have a terrible hand!" or kicking partner under the table is not recommended because of probable ostracism (or worse) by the opponents, and it is not even necessary. You can legally convey this important message by making a *negative 1 ◊ response,* which is conventional and says nothing at all about your holding in the diamond suit. Thus, respond 1 ◊ to partner's 1 ♣ opening bid with any of the following hands:

♠ 7 4 3	♠ K J 8 6
♡ 8 5 4 3 2	♡ 7 4 3
◊ 8 5	◊ K 8 2
♣ 10 4 2	♣ 8 7 2
♠ A J 7 4 2	♠ 6
♡ 5 4 3 2	♡ 9 8 7 6 4 3 2
◊ ——	◊ Q 4 3
♣ 5 4 3 2	♣ 10 5

Since the bidding is at such a low level after the 1 ♣ opening bid and your negative response, you and your partner have ample time to identify your real suits and stop at a reasonable contract.

The first response with positive hands
(8 or more points)

Positive suit responses

With 8 or more points and a suit of *five* or more cards, simply bid your longest suit. In case of ties, bid the *higher-*

ranking suit. Some care must be exercised if your suit is diamonds, for a 1 ◊ response shows 0–7 points—*not* diamonds. Thus, responding 1 ◊ when you don't have 0–7 points and do have diamonds will cause mass confusion. To avoid such a debacle, simply respond *two* diamonds. Also, it is not a particularly good idea to respond in a weak five-card *minor* unless there is no alternative.

Here are some examples of positive suit responses after partner's 1 ♣ opening bid:

♠ 7 3   ♡ A Q 9 6 5   ◊ Q 4 3   ♣ 9 6 2:
Respond 1 ♡.

♠ 10 8 6 4 2   ♡ A K J 7   ◊ A K 3   ♣ 3:
Respond 1 ♠.

♠ K J 8 7 5   ♡ 7   ◊ A Q 8 4 2   ♣ 9 6:
Respond 1 ♠.

♠ 7   ♡ 6 4 3 2   ◊ A 10 7   ♣ A J 4 3 2:
Respond 2 ♣.

♠ 8   ♡ Q 10 8 6 5   ◊ A   ♣ Q 9 7 4 3 2:
Respond 2 ♣.

♠ 7 4   ♡ 6 5 3   ◊ A K J 9 7   ♣ 7 6 2:
Respond 2 ◊.

As always, you should upgrade hands with positive features and downgrade hands with negative features:

♠ 7 4   ♡ K Q 10 9 7   ◊ Q 10 9 8 7   ♣ 3:
Respond 1 ♡. Your 7 points includes two strong suits.

♠ J 8 4 3 2   ♡ Q J   ◊ Q J 4   ♣ J 7 2:
Respond 1 ◊. Your 8 points are all in queens and jacks, and the heart honors are unprotected.

Positive NT responses

After a 1 ♣ opening bid, notrump responses are natural and limited and have the following meaning:

1 NT = 8–10 points, balanced suit distribution.

2 NT = 11–13 points, balanced suit distribution.

3 NT = 14–15 points, balanced suit distribution.*

Some examples (partner opens 1 ♣) :

♠ K Q 9 4   ♡ K 8 3   ◊ Q 10 2   ♣ 5 3 2:
Respond 1 NT.

♠ 6 4   ♡ J 8 6   ◊ A K 4 2   ♣ 9 7 4 3:
Respond 1 NT.

♠ Q 10 3   ♡ Q J 3   ◊ K 4   ♣ J 10 7 4 2:
Respond 1 NT. (Bidding the weak club suit has little to gain.)

♠ K J 3   ♡ A Q 9   ◊ Q 10 4   ♣ 10 7 4 2:
Respond 2 NT.

♠ J 8 6 3   ♡ A 10   ◊ A Q 8 6   ♣ K 10 4:
Respond 3 NT.

Although these responses may conceal one or two four-card major suits, it is not hard to locate a 4–4 major suit fit in the subsequent bidding (as we will see in Chapter 5) .

The impossible negative

There is one hand which is impossible to bid after partner's 1 ♣ opening using the procedures described in this chapter: A

---

* On rare occasions, you may hold 16 or more points and a balanced hand. If so, respond 2 NT and follow with forcing bids that would be inconceivable with a "real" 2 NT response.

positive hand with 4-4-4-1 distribution. For example, suppose you hold

♠ K J 8 7
♡ A 4 3 2
◊ Q 10 8 5
♣ 7

You can't make a positive suit response because you don't have a five-card suit to bid, and you can't make a positive notrump response without balanced suit distribution. Thus, as we saw in Chapter 1, the 4-4-4-1 distribution requires special handling because it is the only unbalanced distribution which does not contain a five-card or longer suit.

The solution for the "impossible" hand is the *impossible negative: Respond 1 ◊, but jump in a new suit or notrump on your next turn.* When partner hears this jump, he will realize that you cannot have a true negative response—after all, who would want to make a jump shift with 0–7 points?—and that you must therefore have the *impossible* negative.

When you do make your jump bid on your next turn, you can take advantage of an unusual opportunity: You can bid three suits at once! Since the impossible negative is made *only* on hands with 4-4-4-1 distribution, the only additional information partner needs in order to have a complete picture is the location of your singleton. Therefore, if the 1 ♣ opener rebids in anything but your singleton suit, jump *in your singleton suit.* It may seem strange to jump in your shortest suit, but what you are really doing is bidding the other three suits simultaneously. Your jump is *forcing,* so you need have no worries about having to play the hand with a singleton trump. If instead partner unobligingly bids your singleton, a jump will sound disconcertingly like a raise and will also use up an excessive number of bidding levels, so *jump in notrump.*

Thus, with 4-4-4-1 distribution and 8 or more points, bid as follows:

STEP 1.   Respond 1 ◊.
STEP 2.   If partner rebids in your singleton suit, *jump*

in notrump. If he rebids anything else,
jump in your singleton suit.

What if partner passes 1 ♦, depriving you of your chance
to complete the picture of the impossible negative? Then you
should get a new partner! It can't possibly be right to stop
bidding when neither you nor your partner has mentioned a
real suit, even if opener's suit happens to be diamonds. Thus,
the 1 ♣ opener will *never* pass a 1 ♦ response.

Some examples of the impossible negative:

♠ K J 8 7   ♡ A 4 3 2   ♦ Q 10 8 5   ♣ 7:
Respond 1 ♦. If partner rebids in clubs, jump in
notrump (for example, rebid 3 NT over 2 ♣). If
partner does anything else, jump in clubs.

♠ A K 7 3   ♡ 4   ♦ A Q 6 3   ♣ Q 4 3 2:
Respond 1 ♦. If partner rebids in hearts, jump in
notrump; if he does anything else, jump in hearts.

In each case, of course, the 1 ♦ response is mendacious, but
partner will forgive the lie (and readjust his picture of your
hand) after you make your jump rebid. Although the point
range for the impossible negative is unlimited, partner will
have such an exact picture of your distribution that the subsequent bidding will be an easy task, as we will see in the next
chapter.

The Precision structure of responses to the 1 ♣ opening
bid is straightforward and has many advantages. An immediate
warning is issued with all poor hands by making a constructive
or negative response. All balanced positive hands are handled
with natural notrump responses. All positive suit responses are
natural and show at least a *five*-card suit, making it easy for
opener to find a good trump suit because he knows that three-
card support will be sufficient. The impossible negative is a
small complication, but is well worth the effort because it con-

veys a precise picture of a hand that would otherwise be difficult to bid.

The first response when the opponents interfere

Although the opponents may be intimidated by partner's 1 ♣ opening, there is no law that requires that they be quiet. Thus, it is possible that your right-hand opponent will interfere with a bid or a takeout double before you get a chance to respond, and Precision has methods to deal appropriately with such occurrences.

After a takeout double

Responding to a 1 ♣ opening followed by a takeout double on your right involves only two changes from the usual procedures.

Pass if you have a negative hand with four or more clubs. Since your right-hand opponent has doubled, partner is sure to get another chance to bid even if you pass. Take advantage of this opportunity to convey additional information to partner by passing with 0–7 points and four or more clubs, and bidding the usual negative 1 ◊ with 0–7 points and no more than three clubs. For example, if partner opens 1 ♣ and the next player doubles, respond 1 ◊ as usual with

> ♠ Q 8 6 4 2
> ♡ 7 2
> ◊ Q 8 3
> ♣ 6 4 2

but *pass* with

> ♠ Q 8 6 4 2
> ♡ 7 2
> ◊ 8 3
> ♣ Q 6 4 2

Redouble with 8 or more points and two four-card majors. The takeout double makes available to you a second bid to describe your hand—redouble. Since positive suit and no-trump responses already show good hands and can easily be made over a takeout double, there is no need to use the redouble solely for strength-showing purposes. Instead, it can serve to clarify your distribution, and the Precision procedure is to redouble with 8 or more points and two four-card majors. A typical example:

> ♠ K Q 7 5
> ♡ J 8 6 2
> ◊ A 4 3
> ♣ 7 2

All other responses after a takeout double retain the standard meaning.

After overcalls through 2 ♠

An overcall in a suit or notrump by your right-hand opponent prevents you from making a negative 1 ◊ response. Therefore, new methods are needed to cope with such interference.

Pass with 0–4 points.

With any hand worth 4 points or less, pass. Partner is assured of another chance to speak.

Bid a new suit or make a negative double with 5–8 points.

With 5–8 points and a *five*-card suit, bid your suit; with the same point count but a *six*-card or longer suit, *jump* in your suit. With any hand worth 5–8 points that does not contain a five-card or longer suit, *double*. This double is conventional and does not express a desire to try and defeat the enemy contract, so partner will not pass unless his own hand justifies a penalty double.

Bid notrump or cue-bid with 9 or more points.

A *single jump in notrump* shows 9–11 points and a balanced hand with at least one stopper in the opponent's suit. If your right-hand opponent overcalls 1 ◊, 1 ♡, or 1 ♠, a *double jump to 3 NT* shows 12–14 points and a balanced hand with at least one stopper in the enemy suit. A *non-jump* notrump response is conventional and forcing to game, and promises at least 9 points and (usually) a good five-card or longer suit. It also shows an unbalanced hand. Finally, with 9 or more points, no stopper in the opponent's suit, and no good five-card or longer suit of your own, request more information from partner by *cue-bidding* the opponent's suit.

Here are some examples to illustrate these principles in action. In each case, partner has opened 1 ♣ and the next player has overcalled 1 ♠.

♠ J 8 6   ♡ 7   ◊ J 7 5 4 3 2   ♣ 10 4 3:
Pass.

♠ 6 4   ♡ 8 7 3   ◊ A Q 9 6 3   ♣ 10 7 4:
Bid 2 ◊, showing a five-card suit and 5–8 points. Precision allows you to compete without the risk of partner getting carried away.

♠ 6 4   ♡ 8 7   ◊ A Q 9 7 6 3   ♣ 10 7 4:
Bid 3 ◊, showing a six-card suit and 5–8 points.

♠ 8   ♡ Q 10 8 4   ◊ A J 7 3   ♣ 8 6 4 2:
Double, showing 5–8 points and no five-card suit. You are not promising any strength in the enemy suit.

♠ Q J 9   ♡ K 10 3   ◊ A 10 5 2   ♣ 5 3 2:
Bid 2 NT.

♠ K Q 10   ♡ K 10 3   ◊ Q 8 6   ♣ K 10 6 5:
Bid 3 NT.

♠ 6   ♡ A K J 7 4 3   ◊ A 4 2   ♣ 6 5 2:
Bid 1 NT, which is forcing and shows 9 or more points. You will bid hearts next time. (An immediate 2 ♡ bid would show a maximum of 8 points.)

♠ A Q 7 6 5   ♡ K 6 4 3   ◊ 5 3 2   ♣ 7:
> *Bid* 1 NT. A double would be negative, not for
> penalties. Unless partner shows a heart suit, you will
> proceed to 3 NT.

♠ 6 4 3   ♡ K 10 7   ◊ K 10 3   ♣ A Q 4 2:
> *Bid* 2 ♠, showing 9 or more points and no clear idea
> what to do—no stopper in the enemy suit and no long
> suit of your own.

Overcalls of 2 NT or higher

In Precision, special methods are recommended for dealing
with interference at the level of 2 NT or higher. These procedures are somewhat complex, however, so the details will be
postponed until the Appendix. As a substitute, you can use the
following procedures: double for penalties; bid 3 NT with
about 9–12 points and at least one good stopper in the opponent's suit, planning to play there unless partner has other
ideas; bid a new good five-card or longer suit if game appears
probable (this now becomes an unlimited bid and is forcing
if below game) ; and cue-bid the enemy suit as a strong takeout.

Preemptive bids are difficult to contend with in any system, and you will have to concede an occasional loss to the
opponents' competitive tactics. Using the double for penalties
at the 2 NT level or higher will make an opponent think
twice about risking an unsound preempt in order to harass you
(and think three times in the future if he tries it and suffers a
sizable penalty) . One final tip: Since partner is not required
to bid again with a minimum if you pass, try and find some
bid with 9 good points or more; but *don't* bid with scanty
values just because partner opened 1 ♣. After a preempt, give
up on finding a part score and enter the fray only if you see a
reasonable chance for at least a game—or a lucrative penalty.

The 1 ♣ opening bid and the first response

Opening bid:
   1 ♣ = 16 or more points; may be shaded slightly with a
      powerful two-suiter.

   Open 2 NT with 22-23 points and balanced suit distribution.

First response:
   1 ◊ = 0–7 points.

   1 ♡, 1 ♠, 2 ♣, 2 ◊ = 8 or more points, at least five cards
      in bid suit. With two five-card or two six-card suits,
      responder chooses the higher-ranking suit.

   2 ♡, 2 ♠ = Six-card suit; 4–7 points, mostly in bid suit.

   3 ♣, 3 ◊, 3 ♡, 3 ♠ = Seven-card suit; 4–7 points, mostly
      in bid suit.

   1 NT = 8–10 points, balanced suit distribution.

   2 NT = 11–13 points, balanced suit distribution.

   3 NT = 14–15 points, balanced suit distribution.

   The Impossible Negative: With 4-4-4-1 distribution and 8
      or more points, (1) respond 1 ◊ ; (2) if partner rebids
      in your singleton, *jump* in notrump; if partner does
      anything else, *jump* in your singleton.

First response after a takeout double:
   Pass = 0–7 points, at least 4 clubs.

   Redouble = 8 or more points, two four-card major suits.

Other responses are unchanged.

First response after an overcall through 2 ♠:
Pass = 0–4 points.

Non-jump new suit = 5–8 points, five cards in bid suit.

Jump in new suit = 5–8 points, six cards in bid suit.

Double = 5–8 points, no five-card or longer suit. *Not* a
    penalty double.

Non-jump notrump response = at least 9 points. Forcing
    to game; usually a good five-card or longer suit.

Single jump in notrump = 9–11 points, balanced suit
    distribution, at least one stopper in opponent's suit.

Double jump to 3 NT over 1 ◇, 1 ♡, or 1 ♠ overcall =
    12–14 points, balanced suit distribution, at least one
    stopper in opponent's suit.

Cue-bid = 9 or more points, *no* stopper in opponent's
    suit, no good five-card or longer suit.

First response after an overcall of 2 NT or higher:
These methods are somewhat complex and will be
    discussed in the Appendix. A possible substitute:
    Double for penalties; 3 NT = natural, to play; New
    suit = natural, probable game, forcing if below the
    level of game; Cue-bid = strong takeout.

REVIEW QUIZ

PART I.

You are the dealer. What call do you make with each of the following hands?

1] ♠ A
   ♡ AKQJ743
   ◇ KQ103
   ♣ 8

2] ♠ KJ8
   ♡ KQ63
   ◇ A1042
   ♣ K6

3] ♠ AKQ
   ♡ KQJ6
   ◇ KQ7
   ♣ Q104

4] ♠ AKJ65
   ♡ AK1073
   ◇ 85
   ♣ 2

5] ♠ QJ6
   ♡ QJ42
   ◇ KQJ
   ♣ KJ3

PART II.

Partner opens 1 ♣. What is your response with each of the following hands? (The opponents are silent.)

6] ♠ 432
   ♡ 5432
   ◇ 432
   ♣ 432

7] ♠ AQJ74
   ♡ K63
   ◇ 62
   ♣ 842

8] ♠ AQ86
   ♡ J63
   ◇ Q93
   ♣ 1076

9] ♠ Q106
   ♡ K3
   ◇ QJ6
   ♣ Q8432

10] ♠ 7
    ♡ KQJ863
    ◇ 1076
    ♣ 1054

11] ♠ 8
    ♡ KQ84
    ◇ A632
    ♣ Q1095

12] ♠ 963
    ♡ 74
    ◇ 63
    ♣ AQ10854

13] ♠ Q107
    ♡ AQ96
    ◇ J1042
    ♣ K10

14] ♠ KJ109843
    ♡ 763
    ◇ 52
    ♣ 7

15] ♠ A53
    ♡ K84
    ◇ AKJ632
    ♣ 10

PART III.

Partner opens 1 ♣ and your right-hand opponent takes the action shown. What call do you make in each case?

16] *Opponent's Bid 1 ♡*
♠ A J 8 6 5
♡ 7 4
♦ A K 3 2
♣ Q 7

17] *Opponent's Bid* Double
♠ K Q J 9
♡ 6 4 3 2
♦ A J 7
♣ 10 9

18] *Opponent's Bid 1 ♠*
♠ 6 4
♡ A Q 10 9 7
♦ 9 6 4 2
♣ 10 7

19] *Opponent's Bid 1 ♡*
♠ 8 7 3
♡ 10 6 2
♦ 6 4 3
♣ Q 9 7 4

20] *Opponent's Bid 1 ♠*
♠ K J 7
♡ A J 6
♦ 10 9 4 2
♣ J 10 4

21] *Opponent's Bid 1 ♡*
♠ A J 8
♡ 6 4 3
♦ A 10 9 7
♣ K 4 3

22] *Opponent's Bid* Double
♠ A J 7 6 5
♡ 8 3
♦ 6 4
♣ A 6 5 2

23] *Opponent's Bid 2 ♡*
♠ A K Q 7 6 5
♡ 7 3
♦ 9 6 3
♣ Q 10

24] *Opponent's Bid 1 ♡*
♠ K 10 8 6
♡ 7 5
♦ A 10 7 2
♣ 6 5 3

25] *Opponent's Bid 3 ♡*
♠ A 4
♡ K Q 10 6
♦ 4 3 2
♣ 9 7 4 3

Solutions

1] *One club.* The forcing 1 ♣ opening includes strong two-bids.
2] *One club.* A minimum 1 ♣ opening.
3] *Two notrump.* Shows 22–23 points and balanced suit distribution.
4] *One club.* You have 15 points, but the strong 5-5 is sufficient compensation. With ♠ J 8 7 6 5   ♡ K 10 8 7 3   ♦ A K ♣ A, however, you would open 1 ♠; these long suits are too weak to warrant extra optimism.
5] *One notrump.* You have just 16 points, and the scarcity of aces and kings should warn you to devalue your hand. (Compare this with the hand in problem 2.)

6] *One diamond.* Tempting though it may be, don't pass! Partner will not accept any excuses if he has a strong two-bid.

7] *One spade.* Shows at least 5 spades and 8 or more points.

8] *One notrump.* Shows 8–10 points and balanced suit distribution.

9] *One notrump.* Much more descriptive than bidding the weak club suit.

10] *Two hearts.* A typical two-level constructive response.

11] *One diamond.* The "impossible negative" with 4-4-4-1 distribution and 8 or more points. If partner rebids in spades, jump in notrump; if he does anything else, jump in spades.

12] *One diamond.* A 2 ♣ response would promise 8 or more points; a 3 ♣ response would show a seven-card suit.

13] *Two notrump.* Shows 11-13 points and a balanced hand.

14] *Three spades.* Promises a seven-card suit and 4–7 points.

15] *Two diamonds.* A 1 ◊ response would be negative. Slam is very likely, but there is no hurry at this point.

16] *One notrump.* Forcing to game and showing 9 or more points and an unbalanced hand. You will bid spades next time. (An immediate 1 ♠ response would show 5–8 points.)

17] *Redouble.* Shows 8 or more points and two four-card majors.

18] *Two hearts.* Shows 5–8 points and a five-card suit. Precision lets you get in there and fight!

19] *Pass.* After an overcall, the pass shows 0–4 points. Partner is assured of another turn.

20] *Two notrump.* Promises 9–11 points and at least one spade stopper.

21] *Two hearts.* With 9 or more points, no good suit of your own, and no stopper in the enemy suit, select the cue-bid.

22] *One spade.* Retains its usual positive meaning after a takeout double. Change the ace of spades to a small spade and you would pass, which would show 0–7 points and at least four clubs.

23] *Two notrump.* Similar in meaning to a 1 NT response over a one-level overcall: Forcing to game with 9 or more points and a probable good suit of your own. You will bid spades next time.

24] *Double.* Negative, showing 5–8 points and no five-card or longer suit.

25] *Double.* At the 2 NT level or higher, use the double for penalties. The opponents will deeply regret this particular indiscretion!

3

Bidding after a 1♣ opening
and a 1♦ response

SOME HIGHLY ARTIFICIAL SYSTEMS involve so many peculiar bids that it would take a Sherlock Holmes to deduce what was going on during the auction. Precision, however, usually follows the straightforward approach of bidding long and strong suits and not mentioning short and weak ones. As our first look at such refreshing simplicity, let's consider the recommended procedures following a 1 ♣ opening bid and a negative 1 ◊ response.

Notrump rebids by opener

With balanced suit distribution, opener describes his hand by making a natural notrump rebid:

> 1 NT rebid = 16–18 points.
> 2 NT rebid = 19–21 points.
> 3 NT rebid = 24–26 points.

For example, after your 1 ♣ opening and partner's 1 ◊ response, rebid in notrump with:

♠ K J 8 6   ♡ A Q 6 4   ◊ A Q 6   ♣ 7 3:
Rebid 1 NT.

♠ K 3   ♡ K J 6   ◊ A J 10   ♣ A J 7 6 3:
Rebid 1 NT. Balanced suit distribution includes 5-3-3-2 with a five-card *minor*. Strength in all suits is ideal for notrump purposes and minor-suit games require two more tricks than notrump games, so there is no reason to introduce the mediocre club suit.

♠ Q 10 7   ♡ A 9 7 6   ◇ A K J   ♣ A Q 3:
Rebid 2 NT.

♠ A K Q 8   ♡ A 7   ◇ Q J 10 4   ♣ A K Q:
Rebid 3 NT.

Auctions after a 1 NT rebid

Since the 1 NT rebid shows the equivalent of a Goren 1 NT opening, you can use your usual methods for handling the subsequent auction. For example:

Opener	Responder (you)
1 ♣	1 ◇
1 NT	?

♠ K J 8 3   ♡ 4 3   ◇ 9 6 5   ♣ 10 4 3 2:
Pass. You have balanced suit distribution and game is out of reach.

♠ K J 8 6 5   ♡ 7 3 2   ◇ 6   ♣ 8 6 5 2:
Bid 2 ♠. Sign off in your five-card suit with unbalanced suit distribution and no chance for game.*

♠ Q J 8 7   ♡ A 4   ◇ 10 9 6 5   ♣ 8 3 2:
Bid 2 ♣ (the Stayman convention). Your side will have 25 Precision points if partner has a maximum, so you should invite game. Raise a 2 ♠ rebid to 3 ♠ and bid 2 NT over anything else.

The only unusual procedure is the jump in a new suit to show the impossible negative:

♠ A J 8 6   ♡ 7 5 3 2   ◇ 4   ♣ A 10 7 5:
Jump to 3 ◇, completing the description of the impossible negative. If partner rebids 3 NT, indicating no concern about the diamond suit and no interest in a suit contract, respect his decision and pass. If he chooses a trump suit, sign off by making a single raise to game.

* Alternatively, Jacoby Transfer Bids may be used.

If you have extra values for your impossible negative and see slam on the horizon, cue-bidding may be just what the doctor ordered:

Opener	Responder
♠ K Q 3	♠ A J 8 6
♡ A Q J 4	♡ K 9 7 3
◇ 10 7 3	◇ 6
♣ A Q 2	♣ K 10 7 4

The bidding:

Opener	Responder
1 ♣	1 ◇
1 NT	3 ◇¹
3 ♡²	3 ♠³
4 ♣⁴	4 ♡⁵
4 ♠⁶	5 ♣⁷
6 ♡⁸	Pass

¹ "Ignore my original pessimistic response. I have an *impossible* negative: 4-4-1-4 distribution with a singleton diamond."
² "Good! I choose hearts as the trump suit."
³ "O.K., hearts are agreed upon. I have the spade ace and some extra values; are you interested in slam?"
⁴ "Yes, and I have the ace of clubs."
⁵ "I'm out of aces and don't have a great deal in reserve, so I'm agreeable if you want to stop here."
⁶ "No, I like our slam chances very much.* I've got the king of spades."
⁷ "I've got the king of clubs. Does that help?"
⁸ "It sure does! If you have a singleton diamond, the spade ace, the club king, four-card heart support, and

* Because he has a maximum with no wasted values opposite partner's singleton diamond. If opener's spade and diamond holdings were switched, he would properly stop in 4 ♡ because of the disastrous duplication of values in diamonds. Note how the impossible negative helps you determine whether or not your high cards are in the right suits!

extra values, the small slam is sure to be an excellent proposition."

Auctions after 2 NT or 3 NT rebids

Your usual methods can also be used after a higher-level notrump rebid by the 1 ♣ opener. After a 2 NT rebid, for example, 3 ♣ is the Stayman convention; 3 ♡ or 3 ♠ is forcing and shows at least a five-card suit; and 3 NT is a signoff.*

If you have begun an impossible negative, however, you should proceed with caution. A jump in a new suit will get the auction very high in a hurry, so it is preferable to use the Stayman convention:

Opener	Responder (you)
1 ♣	1 ◊
2 NT	?

♠ 6 ♡ K Q 3 2 ◊ K 9 7 4 ♣ 8 6 4 3:
> Bid 3 ♣ (Stayman). Had opener rebid 1 NT, you would have followed with 3 ♠ to show all three of your four-card suits at once. Over a 2 NT rebid, however, a 4 ♠ bid will commit your side to the five-level if partner bids a new suit, and will force opener to rebid 4 NT holding 4-3-3-3 distribution with four spades. Stayman is preferable, for you can raise a 3 ♡ rebid by opener to 4 ♡ and sign off in 3 NT otherwise, and it is very unlikely that you will miss a better contract elsewhere.

With stronger hands, jumping in a suit to show the impossible negative will consume bidding space that might well

---

* Either the Flint convention or Jacoby Transfers may be used to enable responder to stop in three of a suit with a weak hand. Using Jacoby Transfers, responder bids 3 ◊ with a poor hand and a five-card or longer heart suit; opener is forced to bid 3 ♡, and responder passes. Similarly, a 3 ♡ response over the jump to 2 NT is a transfer to 3 ♠. With a good hand and a five-card or longer major suit, responder transfers and then bids again over opener's forced reply. Using the Flint convention, a 3 ◊ response shows a weak hand with a five-card or longer major suit and forces opener to bid 3 ♡, whereupon responder passes or signs off in 3 ♠.

be used more profitably for purposes of slam investigation. Therefore, the Precision procedure is to use all jumps to game after a 2 NT rebid as *natural* bids and to bid Stayman with all "impossible negative" hands. Similarly, if you have an impossible negative and partner surprises you by rebidding 3 NT, do *not* jump in your singleton suit.

Jump rebids in a suit by opener

Suppose you open 1 ♣ with a rockcrusher such as

♠ A
♡ A K Q J 7 4 3
◊ A K 4 3
♣ 8

and partner responds 1 ◊. If he has a terrible hand (as is likely in view of your stellar collection), he will want to pass and get on to the next deal as soon as possible. This understandable attitude will produce a most inelegant result if he allows the auction to end in a part score! You could ensure reaching game by jumping to 4 ♡, but this would use up valuable bidding room that you need to investigate slam prospects.

After a 1 ♣ opening and a 1 ◊ response, therefore, Precision uses the *single jump in a suit* (2 ♡, 2 ♠, 3 ♣, and 3 ◊) to announce proud possession of a strong two-bid. These bids are natural and *forcing* for one round. Thus, with the example hand shown above, rebid 2 ♡; you are assured of another chance to speak. The minimum holding for a jump rebid in a suit is 22 points and a good five-card suit *or* a strong distributional hand worth nine tricks. Examples:

♠ 8   ♡ A K J 10 3   ◊ A K Q 7   ♣ A J 3:
Rebid 2 ♡.

♠ A K Q J 7 6 5   ♡ 6   ◊ A K 9   ♣ J 6:
Rebid 2 ♠.

Subsequent bidding

Since opener's jump rebid in a suit shows a strong two-bid, responder must not pass. His choices are:

Non-jump notrump response (2 NT over 2 ♡ or 2 ♠, 3 NT over 3 ♣ or 3 ◊) = 0–3 points, no more than two-card support.

Single raise = 0–3 points, at least three-card support.

Jump raise = 4–7 points, at least good three-card support.

Non-jump new suit = 4–7 points, at least four cards in bid suit.

Jump in notrump = impossible negative, singleton in opener's suit. Opener should choose the trump suit on his next turn.

Jump in new suit = impossible negative, singleton in bid suit. Agrees on opener's suit as the trump suit.

For example, suppose that the auction proceeds 1 ♣ —— 1 ◊ —— 2 ♡. As responder, what should you do with each of the following hands?

♠ 5 4 3 2   ♡ 6 2   ◊ 7 6 2   ♣ 10 7 6 4:
  Bid 2 NT, just as you would after a strong two-bid in standard bidding. If opener now rebids his suit (3 ♡), *responder may pass* (and you certainly would with this hand!), so opener must jump to 4 ♡ or bid a new suit with game in his own hand.

♠ 5 4 3   ♡ 7 4 3   ◊ 7 6 2   ♣ Q 7 6 4:
  Bid 3 ♡, showing 0–3 points and at least three-card heart support.

♠ K J 7 5   ♡ J 6 3 2   ◊ 8 5   ♣ J 10 6:
  Bid 2 ♠, showing the location of your high cards. You will support hearts next time.

♠ J 6 3 2   ♡ K J 7 5   ◊ 8 5   ♣ J 10 6:
  Jump to 4 ♡, showing 4–7 points and at least good

three-card heart support. The weak spade suit is best forgotten.

♠ K 8 4 2   ♡ 9   ◊ 9 7 5 2   ♣ A Q 4 2:
Jump to 3 NT to show the impossible negative with a singleton in opener's suit. *Opener should designate the trump suit on his next turn* by either bidding a good new four-card or longer suit, or rebidding his first suit if it is solid enough to play opposite a small singleton. Thereafter, the partnership uses normal cue-bidding methods to investigate slam.

♠ K J 6 5   ♡ 10 8 6 2   ◊ 7   ♣ K Q J 10:
Jump to 4 ◊ to show the impossible negative with a singleton diamond. Opener's suit (hearts) is confirmed as the trump suit because responder is known to hold four-card support, so cue-bidding may begin with opener's next bid.

Simple suit rebids by opener

If opener does not have a strong two-bid or a hand qualifying for a notrump rebid, he makes a natural rebid in his longest suit. For example, suppose the auction has proceeded 1 ♣ —— 1 ◊ and you (opener) hold:

♠ A Q 8 6 5   ♡ A K 7 2   ◊ A 8 3   ♣ 4:
Rebid 1 ♠.

♠ A J 7 6 5   ♡ K Q J 10 9   ◊ 6   ♣ A Q:
Rebid 1 ♠. With two five-card or two six-card suits, choose the *higher-ranking* suit.

♠ Q   ♡ K Q 7 6 5   ◊ A   ♣ A Q 7 6 4 3:
Rebid 2 ♣.

♠ K 8 6 4   ♡ A Q 7 5   ◊ A K J 3   ♣ 2:
Rebid 1 ♡. You may not rebid in notrump with

unbalanced suit distribution, but you may bid a four-card *major* suit. Choosing hearts allows responder to mention spades at the one-level.

♠ A K J 7   ♡ J 4 3 2   ◇ A K J 3   ♣ 2:
Rebid 1 ♠. It is best to avoid bidding a weak four-card suit if possible, so prefer the strong spades to the anemic hearts. (However, *don't* bid a four-card *minor*.)

♠ A   ♡ A Q 6 2   ◇ A K 10 7 4   ♣ 8 6 3:
Rebid 2 ◇.

Subsequent bidding

Responder's first bid of 1 ◇ shows 0–7 points, but indicates nothing about his distribution. Therefore, his most important obligation is to help determine the trump suit as quickly as possible, and the first place to look is the suit suggested by opener's rebid.

Responder has 0, 1, or 2-card support.
With no more than two-card support for opener's suit and 0–4 points, pass. True, opener has a strong hand; but with neither points nor support, prospects are decidedly gloomy. With 5–7 points and a five-card or longer suit, bid it; with 5–7 points and no five-card or longer suit, bid notrump as cheaply as possible (1 NT over a 1 ♡ or 1 ♠ rebid, 2 NT over a 2 ♣ or 2 ◇ rebid).

Responder has 3-card or longer support.
With three-card or longer support for opener's suit, pass with a zero or one-point horror and make a single raise with 2–4 points. With 5–7 points and *three*-card support, bid a five-card suit or notrump as cheaply as possible and then support opener's suit on the next round; with 5–7 points and *four*-card or longer support, *jump* raise opener's suit.

Responder has an impossible negative.
As usual, jump in notrump to show an impossible negative

with a singleton in opener's suit. Opener will bid a new four-card or longer suit; rebid his own suit if it is solid and can play opposite a small singleton; and rebid in notrump if a suit contract looks inadvisable. A jump response in a new suit shows an impossible negative with a singleton in the bid suit and designates opener's suit as the trump suit.

Some examples of these highly natural methods are shown below.

Remember to count distribution points when planning to raise partner's suit.

Opener	Responder (you)
1 ♣	1 ◊
1 ♠	?

♠ 6 3   ♡ 8 6 4 2   ◊ Q 8 6 3   ♣ J 4 2:
> *Pass.* You have only 3 points and your spade support is poor.

♠ 8 6 3   ♡ Q 8 6 4   ◊ J 10 4 3   ♣ 7 5:
> *Raise to 2 ♠*, showing 2–4 points and at least three-card spade support. Since your 4 points (counting one point for the doubleton club) is the most partner can expect after a single raise, you should accept a game invitation if one is offered.

♠ 6 3   ♡ A Q 10 8 4   ◊ 10 9 4 2   ♣ 7 6:
> *Bid 2 ♡*, showing 5–7 points and a five-card suit. Pass if partner returns to 2 ♠, raise a 3 ♡ invitation to 4 ♡, and raise a 2 NT invitation to 3 NT.

♠ 6 3   ♡ Q 9 8 7 5   ◊ K 10 4 2   ♣ 5 3:
> *Bid 2 ♡.* Decline any game invitation.

♠ 7 5 3   ♡ A Q 8 6 5   ◊ 8 7 4   ♣ 10 3:
> *Bid 2 ♡*; then bid spades next time to show three-card support.

♠ 7 5 3 2   ♡ A J 7 6 3   ◇ 8 7 3   ♣ 2:
Jump to 3 ♠, showing 5–7 points and four-card
support. You know that a fine spade fit exists; don't
keep partner in the dark by bidding hearts.

♠ 8 7   ♡ A Q 8 6   ◇ J 4 2   ♣ 9 7 6 2:
Bid 1 NT, showing 5–7 points and no five-card or
longer suit. You should pass if partner rebids 2 ♠,
raise a 2 ♡ or 2 ♣ rebid, and raise a 2 NT invitation
to 3 NT.

♠ 8 4 2   ♡ K 10 6 3   ◇ 7 4   ♣ J 8 6 2:
Bid 1 NT; then bid spades next time to show
three-card support. Counting one point for the
diamond doubleton because you plan to raise partner's
suit, your hand is worth 5 points. If partner has a
semi-balanced minimum and passes your 1 NT
response, you will be in a reasonable contract.

♠ 6   ♡ A J 8 4   ◇ Q 9 6 3   ♣ K 10 8 3:
Jump to 2 NT to show the impossible negative with a
singleton in opener's suit. Opener should choose a
trump suit on his next turn if he can, or bid 3 NT if
he does not fancy a suit contract opposite your
announced distribution. If a trump fit is found, slam
can be investigated by means of cue-bids.

♠ 10 8 6 3   ♡ 7   ◇ K Q 6 3   ♣ A J 4 2:
Jump to 3 ♡ to show the impossible negative with a
singleton heart. This fixes spades as the trump suit
and invites opener to begin cue-bidding with extra
values. If opener rebids 3 ♠, give up on slam with
your near-minimum holding and sign off in 4 ♠.

♠ 8 7 6 5   ♡ K J 7 6   ◇ J 10 7 6 5   ♣ ——:
Special care is needed here! Your hand was worth
only 5 points after partner's 1 ♣ opening. Now that
you plan to raise spades, however, you count 5 points

for your club void and your hand improves in value to 10 points. Convey the good news to partner by making a *triple jump* to 4 ♠, showing four-card or longer support and a hand too strong for a double raise.

A detailed discussion of every possible auction after responder's rebid would be so lengthy and tedious that any self-respecting reader would soon switch to canasta. Fortunately, such a boring treatise is unnecessary because Precision is primarily a natural system, and (as you can see from the above examples) the subsequent bidding is straightforward.

Bidding after a 1♣ opening and a 1♦ response

Opener's rebid	Responder's rebid
1 NT = 16–18 points, balanced suit distribution (4-3-3-3, 4-4-3-2, or 5-3-3-2 with a weak five-card *minor* suit).	2 ♣ = Stayman. 2 ♦, 2 ♥, or 2 ♠ = signoff, five-card or longer suit. Jump in new suit = impossible negative, singleton in bid suit.
2 NT = 19–21 points, balanced suit distribution.	3 ♣ = Stayman. Use Stayman with an impossible negative —do **not** jump! 3 ♥ or 3 ♠ = natural, forcing. (Alternatively, 3 ♦ and 3 ♥ may be used as Jacoby Transfers, or 3 ♦ may be used as the Flint convention.)
3 NT = 24–26 points, balanced suit distribution.	Do *not* jump with an impossible negative!*
Jump in new suit (2 ♥, 2 ♠, 3 ♣, or 3 ♦) = at least 22 points and a good five-card or longer suit, or at least nine tricks and a long suit. (A strong two-bid.)	Non-jump notrump response = 0–3 points, no more than two-card support. Single raise = 0–3 points, at least three-card support. Jump raise = 4–7 points, at least good three-card support.

* Use a 4 ♠ response as *modified* Stayman for *any* four-card suit. Modified Stayman will be explained in Chapter 5.

Opener's rebid	Responder's rebid
	Non-jump new suit = 4–7 points, at least four cards in bid suit. **Try to avoid bidding very weak suits.**
	Jump in notrump = impossible negative, singleton in opener's suit.
	Jump in new suit = impossible negative, singleton in bid suit.
Simple suit rebid by opener (1 ♡, 1 ♠, 2 ♣, 2 ◇) = natural, 16–21 points.	Pass = any 0–1 point hand; 2–4 points and at most two-card support.
	Single raise = 2–4 points, at least three-card support.
	Jump raise = 5–7 points, at least four-card support.
	Non-jump new suit = 5–7 points, at least five cards in bid suit.* With three-card support for opener's suit, bid opener's suit on next turn.
	Non-jump notrump response = 5–7 points, no five-card or longer suit. With three-card support for opener's suit, bid opener's suit on next turn.
	Triple raise to 4 ♡ or 4 ♠ = at least four-card support, hand now worth more than 7 points.

---

* Exception: After a 1 ♣ opening, a 1 ◇ response, and a 1 ♡ rebid, responder may bid 1 ♠ with a good four-card spade suit.

PRECISION SYSTEM

Opener's rebid	*Responder's rebid*
	Jump in notrump = impossible negative, singleton in opener's suit.
	Jump in notrump = impossible negative, singleton in opener's suit.

REVIEW QUIZ

PART I.

You open 1 ♣ and partner responds 1 ◊ in each of the following problems. Decide upon your rebid, and plan the subsequent auction after the most probable rebids by responder.

1] ♠ A3
♡ AJ863
◊ KQ8
♣ K63

2] ♠ AKQJ65
♡ AKQ
◊ Q103
♣ 7

3] ♠ A83
♡ A62
◊ 7
♣ AKJ753

4] ♠ AQ86
♡ AQ6
◊ KJ7
♣ 1083

6] ♠ 7
♡ AQJ106
◊ AKQJ
♣ AK7

6] ♠ KJ3
♡ Q32
◊ AQ86
♣ AKQ

7] ♠ 6
♡ AJ1097
◊ AKQJ2
♣ 107

8] ♠ 8
♡ QJ42
◊ AK63
♣ AQ108

PART II.

You are responder in each of the following problems. Partner has opened 1 ♣, you have responded 1 ◊, and opener has made the rebid shown. What call do you make?

9] *Opener's Rebid* 1 ♠
♠ 8
♡ KJ86
◊ AQ102
♣ Q842

10] *Opener's Rebid* 1 ♡
♠ 865
♡ J832
◊ 109865
♣ 7

11] *Opener's Rebid* 1 ♡
♠ –
♡ A865
◊ 9642
♣ Q8653

12] *Opener's Rebid* 1 NT
♠ 9863
♡ 10
◊ KQ63
♣ A972

13] *Opener's Rebid* 1 ♡
♠ AJ1064
♡ 72
◊ 65
♣ J1082

14] *Opener's Rebid* 2 NT
♠ KQ86
♡ 7
◊ K863
♣ J1065

15] *Opener's Rebid* 2 ♠
♠ 8
♡ KJ106
◊ 10975
♣ A1043

16] *Opener's Rebid* 2 ♠
♠ 85
♡ 6532
◊ 632
♣ 9764

17] *Opener's Rebid* 2 ♣
♠ AJ86
♡ Q63
◊ 8432
♣ 93

18] *Opener's Rebid* 1 ♡
♠ 5
♡ K Q 6 3
◇ A 9 4 2
♣ 10 7 4 3

19] *Opener's Rebid* 1 NT
♠ 7
♡ K 8 6 5 3
◇ 7 4 2
♣ 8 7 5 3

20] *Opener's Rebid* 1 ♠
♠ Q 8 6 3
♡ 8 3
◇ A 8 5
♣ 8 7 6 5

21] *Opener's Rebid* 2 ♠
♠ K J 7 6
♡ 8 6 5 3 2
◇ 8 6 3
♣ 7

22] *Opener's Rebid* 2 NT
♠ 8 7 5
♡ Q 8 6 4
◇ J 7 6 5
♣ 4 3

23] *Opener's Rebid* 1 ♡
♠ Q 9 7 2
♡ 8 6
◇ 8 6 5 4
♣ 9 4 3

24] *Opener's Rebid* 1 ♡
♠ Q 6 5 3
♡ 7
◇ K 8 4 3
♣ 7 4 3 2

25] *Opener's Rebid* 3 NT
♠ Q 6 5
♡ 8 4 3
◇ J 10 8 7
♣ K 10 5

Solutions

1] *One heart.* With a minimum, you intend to pass if partner bids a new suit or 1 NT, or raises hearts. If he jumps in a new suit to show an impossible negative with a singleton in the bid suit (and therefore heart support), rebid 3 ♡ to indicate a minimum and lack of interest in slam. If instead partner jumps to 2 NT, showing an impossible negative with a singleton heart, bid 3 NT.

2] *Two spades.* If partner rebids 2 NT, give him a chance to stop short of game by rebidding 3 ♠. If instead he bids a new suit, rebid spades. If responder's rebid is 3 NT, showing an impossible negative with a singleton spade, designate spades as the trump suit by rebidding 4 ♠; while if partner shows an impossible negative with spade support by jumping in a new suit, you may begin to cue-bid. (If partner happens to bid 4 ◇, showing his singleton where you need it most, you can go straight to Blackwood.)

3] *Two clubs.* If partner rebids 2 ♡ or 2 ♠, showing 5–7 points and at least a five-card suit, invite game by raising to three. If instead he rebids 2 ◇ or 2 NT, return to 3 ♣; game in notrump is unlikely opposite a maximum of 7 points. If partner jumps to 3 NT, showing an impossible negative with a singleton club, your best bet is to pass. Partner may be surprised, but the hands fit very poorly and he would need an enormous hand to produce a slam. Any other impossible negative shows club support, so you should start cue-bidding your side-suit aces.

4] *One notrump.* Most auctions will proceed just as though you had opened with a Goren 1 NT. For example, pass a 2 NT invitation; bid 2 ♠ over a Stayman 2 ♣ rebid. If instead responder jumps to 3 ♠ to show an impossible negative with a singleton spade, bid 3 NT; after any other impossible negative, bid 3 ♠.

5] *Two hearts.* If partner raises to 3 ♡, sign off in 4 ♡. If he jumps to 4 ♡, showing 4–7 points and (probably) ♡ K 3 2 or better, try for slam by bidding 5 ♣ (you want partner to realize that the club queen is a treasure but the spade queen or king is not). If partner bids 2 NT, 2 ♠, or 3 ♣, show your diamonds. Finally, if partner has an impossible negative, either hearts or diamonds will make a fine trump suit depending on the location of his singleton. If he bids 3 NT, name the trump suit by bidding 4 ◊ and cue-bid thereafter; if he jumps in a suit, start cue-bidding immediately (hearts being agreed upon as the trump suit).

6] *Two notrump.* Remember that if responder jumps to game over a 2 NT or 3 NT rebid, this is natural and *not* the impossible negative.

7] *One heart.* With two five-card or two six-card suits, bid the higher-ranking suit. Over most actions by responder, you will bid diamonds twice to show a strong two-suiter. If, however, partner raises to 2 ♡, invite game by bidding 3 ♡; and if instead his first rebid is 3 ♡, raise to 4 ♡.

8] *One heart.* Don't bid a four-card minor. Rebid 1 NT over a 1 ♠ bid by partner; otherwise, pass quickly in any playable part-score contract unless responder shows an impossible negative.

9] *Two notrump.* Shows an impossible negative with a singleton in opener's suit. You will pass a 3 NT rebid, cue-bid the diamond ace over a 3 ♣ or 3 ♡ rebid to show extra values, and raise 3 ◊ to 5 ◊ (showing extra values but no side-suit ace to cue-bid).

10] *Two hearts.* Shows 2–4 points and at least three-card heart support. Counting three points for the club singleton, your hand is worth 4 points, so you will go on to game in the unlikely event that opener suggests such a possibility.

11] *Four hearts.* Counting 5 points for the spade void when raising partner's suit, the market value of your hand zooms to 11 points. Let partner know by making a triple raise.

12] *Three hearts.* Shows an impossible negative with a singleton heart. You will pass a 3 NT rebid or make a single raise of any new suit that opener selects, showing no extra values.

13] *One spade.* Shows 5–7 points and a five-card suit. Pass a minimum rebid such as 1 NT or 2 ♡, but raise a 2 ♠ rebid to 3 ♠.

14] *Three clubs.* The Stayman convention. *Don't* jump after a 2 NT or 3 NT rebid with an impossible negative. You will raise a 3 ♠ rebid to 4 ♠ and bid 3 NT otherwise.

15] *Three notrump.* The impossible negative with a singleton in opener's suit. After opener chooses a trump suit, cue-bid your club ace. (If he selects clubs, raise.)

16] *Two notrump.* Shows 0–3 points and at most two-card support for opener's suit. You will happily pass if opener rebids 3 ♠ (or 4 ♠), but must continue to bid if he bids a new suit. (Your best choice is to bid spades as cheaply as possible since you have already denied three-card support.)

17] *Two notrump.* Shows 5–7 points and no five-card or longer suit. If opener shows a four-card spade suit by bidding 3 ♠, raise to 4 ♠.

18] *Two spades.* This impossible negative shows heart support and hence fixes hearts as the trump suit. You will make a minimum rebid in hearts on your next turn to indicate no extra values.

19] *Two hearts.* Sign off in your five-card major suit with no chance for game.

20] *Three spades.* Shows 5–7 points and at least four-card spade support. Partner will probably sign off in 4 ♠; if he happens to make a slam try, cue-bid your diamond ace.

21] *Four spades.* Shows 4–7 points and at least three-card support, probably including an honor. There is no good reason to bid hearts; a suit fit has been found and a strong two-bidder is interested in honor strength, not five to an eight-spot.

22] *Pass.* Game is out of reach despite opener's fine hand.

23] *Pass.* You have only 2 points and poor heart support.

24] *One notrump.* A suit response would promise a five-card suit. You have "impossible negative" distribution but a genuine negative in terms of points, so there is no reason to do anything unusual.

25] *Pass.* Slam is unlikely even if partner has a 26-point maximum, and notrump looks like an ideal contract.

The answers to this quiz have been presented at some length to show that auctions after 1 ♣—1 ◇ are natural and straightforward. To be sure, the impossible negative is an exception, but it provides such a precise picture of responder's hand that it is both simple and enjoyable to use. Thus, you should be able to deal accurately with just about any situation that you are likely to encounter after an opening 1 ♣ bid and a 1 ◇ response.

4

Bidding
after a 1♣ opening and
a constructive response

IF YOU WALK around the table and take a look at your partner's hand during the bidding, the opponents are likely to do something drastic. If you remain in your seat and partner makes a constructive response, you have just about as much of an advantage—and the opponents can do nothing except suffer in silence.

Opener's rebid after a constructive response

A constructive response paints an admirably precise picture. If you open 1 ♣ and partner responds 2 ♡ or 2 ♠, you know that he has a six-card suit and 4–7 points, most of which are in the bid suit (or seven to the jack). A constructive response of 3 ♣, 3 ◊, 3 ♡, or 3 ♠ is similar except that responder guarantees possession of a seven-card suit (or eight to the jack). With all of this valuable information at your disposal, you are in an excellent position to determine the best contract, and you can exploit your advantage by making judicious use of the following bidding weaponry:

> *Pass if there is no chance for game.* Responder has a good suit, so *don't* bid just to try for a better part score even if your support is poor.

> *Raise partner's suit.* A raise to 3 ♡, 3 ♠, 4 ♣, or 4 ◊ is invitational, asking partner to pass with a minimum and proceed to game with a maximum. A raise to game is a signoff.

Sign off in game. A rebid of 3 NT or game in a new suit is a signoff.

Bid a new suit. The bid of a new suit below the level of game is *forcing* and asks responder to raise with three-card or better support. With poor support, responder cue-bids a new suit below 3 NT or bids 3 NT with a maximum and rebids his own suit with a minimum.

Make a forcing 2 NT rebid with a strong hand and good support for partner's suit. If partner responds 2 ♡ or 2 ♠ and you have a hand with good support for his suit, you can investigate game or slam prospects by rebidding 2 NT. This bid is *forcing,* agrees on partner's suit as the trump suit, and asks partner to cue-bid a *singleton or void suit* if he has one. If he cannot oblige, partner rebids his suit.

Let's take a look at these procedures in action. In each of the following examples, you have opened the bidding with 1 ♣ and partner has made the constructive response shown.

Responder's bid

1] 2 ♡   ♠ A Q 8 6   ♡ 7   ◇ A K 8 4   ♣ K J 3 2: Pass. Partner has a good suit, and game is out of reach. Looking around for a better part score is likely to enrich only the opponents.

2] 2 ♠   ♠ A K 3   ♡ A 7 5   ◇ A 10 4   ♣ A 8 6 3: Bid 3 NT. Partner should *not* make a constructive response on six to the jack or worse, so you can count nine probable tricks.

3] 3 ♠   ♠ K Q J   ♡ A 7 4 3   ◇ A 6 3   ♣ A K Q: Bid 4 NT (Blackwood). You can tell

Responder's bid

that partner has seven spades to the ace, giving your side twelve top tricks. You will follow with 5 NT, stopping in 6 NT if partner has no kings and bidding 7 NT if he has one king.

4]   2 ♠   ♠ A J 8 ♡ A 9 3 ◇ A K Q 4 3 ♣ 5 2: Bid 4 ♠. With so many top tricks, you have a good chance for game even if partner has nothing but six spades to the king.

5]   2 ♠   ♠ A J 8 ♡ Q J 3 ◇ A Q J 6 5 ♣ K 4: Bid 3 ♠, inviting partner to continue to game with a maximum. Side-suit queens and jacks are likely to be of minimal value opposite a one-suited hand, so you will need help to produce a game.

6]   2 ♠   ♠ 4 3 ♡ A K 6 5 ◇ A K 7 3 ♣ A K 2· Bid 4 ♠. If partner lacks a side-suit entry, you will have great difficulty in a notrump contract. Avoid 3 NT contracts with a poor fit for responder's suit.

7]   3 ♣   ♠ 6 5 3 ♡ A K Q J 7 4 2 ◇ A K 10 ♣ ——: Sign off in 4 ♡. With partner's strength primarily in clubs, slam is unlikely to be a good bet, so don't prolong the issue. Had partner responded 2 ♠, slam would be a distinct possibility and you would rebid 3 ♡ (forcing) to leave room for exploration.

Responder's bid

8]   2 ♡   ♠ A 7 6 3   ♡ A Q J 4   ◇ A K Q 3   ♣ 2:
Bid 2 NT. This bid is forcing, agrees on responder's suit as the trump suit, and asks him to describe his hand further by cue-bidding a singleton or void suit. You definitely want to be in slam if responder has a spade singleton or void along with his good six-card heart suit, but otherwise will only invite slam by cue-bidding the spade ace.

Responder's rebid

If you have made a constructive response to partner's 1 ♣ opening bid, remember that opener will not bid again unless there is a chance for game. If he bids a new suit, clarify your hand by raising with three-card or longer support; if you cannot raise, cue-bid a new suit below 3 NT or bid notrump with a maximum and rebid your suit with a minimum. If your response was 2 ♡ or 2 ♠ and opener rebids 2 NT, you are asked to cue-bid a singleton or void suit if you have one; otherwise, you should rebid your suit. Any game bid by opener is a signoff, and a raise of your suit below game is invitational.

For example, suppose that partner has opened 1 ♣ and you have made a constructive 2 ♡ response. If opener makes the rebid shown, what call would you make with each of the following hands?

Opener's rebid

1]   3 ♡   ♠ 7 5   ♡ Q 10 6 4 3 2   ◇ Q 6 3   ♣ 8 4:
Pass. You have a 4-point minimum.

2]   3 ♡   ♠ 7 5   ♡ A Q 9 8 6 5   ◇ 8 3 2   ♣ 10 5:
Bid 4 ♡.

Opener's rebid

3] 4 ♠   ♠ —— ♡ K J 10 9 6 3 ◊ Q 10 4 2
    (or 3 NT,   ♣ 7 6 2:   Pass. You have told your
    or 4 ♡)   story and partner has chosen the final
                     contract.

4] 2 ♠   ♠ 8 6 3 ♡ K J 9 7 4 3 ◊ 6 3 2 ♣ 7:
                     Bid 3 ♠. Show three-card or longer
                     support for opener's suit.

5] 2 ♠   ♠ 6 3 ♡ A J 10 8 7 5 ◊ 7 3 ♣ Q 4 2:
                     Bid 3 ♣. With poor support for
                     opener's suit, cue-bid a new suit with
                     maximum and rebid your suit with a
                     minimum.

6] 2 NT   ♠ 8 6 5 ♡ A 10 9 6 5 3 ◊ Q J 4 ♣ 7:
                     Bid 3 ♣. Opener has agreed upon
                     hearts as the trump suit and would
                     like to know if you have a side-suit
                     singleton or void. Change a small
                     spade to a small club and you would
                     rebid 3 ♡, showing no singleton or
                     void.

An important reminder: Don't make a constructive response if your suit is weak; it should include at least one of the
top three honors (*or* an extra card in the suit if it is headed
by the jack) . Partner will be counting upon you to have a good
suit, and the opponents are likely to have the last laugh if you
disappoint him.

Bidding after a 1♣ opening and a constructive response

Opener should pass with no chance for game, even if his support for responder's suit is poor.

A raise by opener to 3 ♡, 3 ♠, 4 ♣, or 4 ◊ is invitational. Responder should pass with a minimum and continue to game with a maximum.

Any game bid by opener is a signoff. This inclues 3 NT, a game bid in a new suit, or a raise to game of responder's suit.

A bid of a new suit below game by opener is natural and forcing. Responder is asked to bid as follows:

>Three-card or longer support for opener's suit: Raise opener's suit.

>Poor support, maximum hand: Cue-bid a new suit below 3 NT, or bid 3 NT.

>Poor support, minimum hand: Rebid own suit.

A rebid of 2 NT by opener after a 2 ♡ or 2 ♠ response is forcing and agrees on responder's suit as the trump suit. Responder is asked to bid as follows:

>Responder has a singleton or void suit: Cue-bid this suit.

>No singleton or void suit: Rebid own suit.

REVIEW QUIZ

PART I.

You have opened 1 ♣ and partner has made the constructive response shown in each of the following problems. What call do you make?

1] Responder's Bid 3 ♡
- ♠ A Q 3
- ♡ 4 3
- ◇ A K J 4 3
- ♣ K Q 3

2] Responder's Bid 2 ♡
- ♠ A Q J 9 8 3
- ♡ 7
- ◇ A K J 8 6
- ♣ 2

3] Responder's Bid 2 ♡
- ♠ Q 10 7 4 3
- ♡ 5
- ◇ A J 6
- ♣ A K Q 3

4] Responder's Bid 2 ♠
- ♠ Q 8 3
- ♡ A Q J 6 3
- ◇ K 2
- ♣ A K 6

5] Responder's Bid 2 ♠
- ♠ K Q 4 2
- ♡ 8 7 6 3
- ◇ A K Q 2
- ♣ A

6] Responder's Bid 3 ♣
- ♠ A K Q 10 9 8 5
- ♡ 5 4 3
- ◇ A K J
- ♣ --

7] Responder's Bid 2 ♡
- ♠ A K 8
- ♡ K J 4
- ◇ K Q J 7
- ♣ K 7 6

PART II.

Partner has opened 1 ♣ and your first response and his rebid are shown in each of the following problems. What call do you make?

8] Your Response 2 ♡
Opener's Rebid 3 ♡
- ♠ 6
- ♡ K J 10 9 7 3
- ◇ Q 10 4 2
- ♣ 4 2

9] Your Response 2 ♠
Opener's Rebid 2 NT
- ♠ K J 10 6 4 2
- ♡ 7
- ◇ 7 4 3
- ♣ 10 6 2

10] Your Response 2 ♡
Opener's Rebid 2 ♠
- ♠ 4 3
- ♡ Q J 10 6 4 3
- ◇ Q 10 3
- ♣ 6 3

11] *Your Response* 3 ♠
   Opener's Rebid 3 NT
   ♠ K J 8 7 6 3 2
   ♡ 6 5 4
   ◇ J
   ♣ 8 2

12] *Your Response* 2 ♠
   Opener's Rebid 3 ♡
   ♠ A Q 10 6 4 3
   ♡ 7
   ◇ 8 6
   ♣ J 9 3 2

13] *Your Response* 3 ♣
   Opener's Rebid 3 ♡
   ♠ 7 3
   ♡ 8 6 2
   ◇ 6
   ♣ K Q 10 7 4 3 2

14] *Your Response* 3 ♡
   Opener's Rebid 4 ♠
   ♠ –
   ♡ A J 9 8 7 4 3
   ◇ 6 3 2
   ♣ 10 7 3

15] *Your Response* 2 ♡
   Opener's Rebid 2 NT
   ♠ 7 3
   ♡ Q 10 9 8 6 4
   ◇ A J 3
   ♣ 9 7

Solutions

1] *Four hearts.* Game is worth bidding opposite a good seven-card suit, but 3 NT would be a poor choice. If the opponents have the heart ace and are not obliging enough to play it on the first round of the suit, you may never be able to reach dummy and run the heart suit.

2] *Two spades.* Partner will raise with three-card or better support, cue-bid a new suit with a maximum and poor support, or rebid his suit with a minimum and poor support. He must *not* pass your forcing bid!

3] *Pass.* Don't bid just to try and find a better part score.

4] *Three spades.* Invite partner to proceed to game with a maximum.

5] *Two notrump.* Slam is assured if partner has a void or singleton heart, but will require careful exploration otherwise. The 2 NT rebid fixes spades as the trump suit and caters to both possibilities.

6] *Four spades.* A signoff.

7] *Four hearts.* There is a fine chance for game and none for slam.

8] *Four hearts.* You have a near-maximum, so accept partner's invitation.

9] *Three hearts.* The 2 NT rebid agrees on spades as the trump suit and asks you to cue-bid a void or singleton suit. Change a small club to a small heart and you would rebid 3 ♠, showing a minimum with no singleton or void.

10] *Three hearts.* Shows a minimum with poor spade support. You may not pass; the rebid of a new suit below the level of game is forcing.

11] *Pass.* It may seem strange to play in notrump with a seven-card suit, but partner knows what you have and there is no reason to disturb his signoff. Opener's hand is

♠ A Q 5
♡ A 3 2
◊ A 6 3 2
♣ Q J 3;

you have nine sure tricks in notrump and four probable losers in spades.

12] *Four clubs.* Shows a maximum hand with poor support for opener's suit. If opener rebids 4 ♡ or 4 ♠, pass.

13] *Four hearts.* A single raise of opener's suit promises three-card or longer support.

14] *Pass.* You have shown your hand and must respect partner's signoff.

15] *Three hearts.* Shows a hand with no void or singleton.

5

Bidding
after a 1♣ opening and
a positive response

VIRTUE MAY BE its own reward, but large numbers on your side of the score sheet are far more profitable. When you open the bidding with 1 ♣ and partner makes a positive response, your partnership must have at least 24 points, so lucrative results (such as game and slam) are clearly visible on the horizon.

Positive NT responses

A positive notrump response to your 1 ♣ opening bid limits partner's hand so precisely that you will find it easy to confound your opponents with highly accurate bidding. Let's consider each of these responses in turn.

Auctions after a positive 1 NT response

A 1 NT response to your 1 ♣ opening bid shows balanced suit distribution and 8–10 points. (As always, keep in mind that only high-card points are included in the total unless a suit is being raised.) The following choices are available to you for your rebid:

> *Bid a new good five-card or longer suit.* This bid is *forcing* and asks partner to raise with three-card or longer support. With only two-card support, partner should show a four-card major if he has one and return to notrump if he does not. (Since partner has balanced suit distribution, he cannot have any voids or singletons.)

> *Make a natural notrump raise.* A raise to 2 NT is invitational to 3 NT; a jump to 3 NT is a signoff; and a raise to

4 NT is invitational to 6 NT. With a relatively balanced minimum hand and no chance for slam, prefer a notrump raise to rebidding a five-card *minor* suit; game in notrump requires *two* fewer tricks than game in a minor.

Make a Stayman 2 ♣ bid. Since the 1 NT response may conceal one or two four-card major suits, a 2 ♣ rebid by opener is Stayman and asks responder to unveil a four-card major if he has one.* If not, responder bids 2 ◊.

Here are some examples of these rebids:

Opener (you)	Responder
1 ♣	1 NT
?	

♠ K J 8   ♡ K Q 6   ◊ A 8 6 4   ♣ K 10 2:
Invite game in notrump by raising to 2 NT. You will never pass a 1 NT response even with a rock-bottom minimum such as this one, for you belong in game if partner has 9 or 10 points.

♠ K J 8   ♡ K Q 6   ◊ A Q 8 6   ♣ K 10 2:
Sign off in 3 NT. Your 18 points plus partner's 8 equals 26, one more than the Precision minimum needed to bid game, and slam is out of reach.

♠ K J 8 7   ♡ K 7   ◊ A J 10 4   ♣ A 10 7:
Bid 2 ♣ (Stayman). If partner bids 2 ♠, proceed directly to 4 ♠; your hand is worth 17 points (counting one point for the doubleton heart when raising partner's suit). If instead partner responds 2 ◊ or 2 ♡, your hand is worth only 16 points and

---

* With two four-card majors, responder should bid the stronger major. If opener denies support by returning to notrump, responder then shows the other major.

you should bid just 2 NT, inviting partner to continue to 3 NT with a maximum.

♠ A K J 7 6   ♡ K 8 3   ◇ A Q 3   ♣ 4 2:
Bid 2 ♠, which is forcing, shows a good five-card or longer suit, and asks partner to raise to 3 ♠ with three or more spades. Game must be a good bet once a satisfactory suit fit has been detected, so partner's single raise is forcing; you should cue-bid with substantial extra values and sign off in 4 ♠ with a minimum hand such as this one. If instead partner bids 2 NT over 2 ♠, raise to 3 NT.

♠ 8 3   ♡ K Q 7 2   ◇ A K 9 8 5 4   ♣ A:
Bid 2 ◇. Partner will raise with three-card or longer diamond support; otherwise, he will bid a four-card major suit if he has one. If he strikes oil by bidding 2 ♡, let him know by raising to 3 ♡ (forcing to game). If the fates are unkind and he bids 2 ♠ or 2 NT, bid 3 ♡ to further describe your hand and offer him a choice between 3 NT and 5 ◇.

As you can see, bidding after a positive 1 NT response is natural and straightforward. Keep the following guidelines in mind:

1] Responder cannot have a void, singleton, or good five-card or longer major suit for his 1 NT response. (He might have a weak five-card minor.)

2] A 2 ♣ rebid by opener is the Stayman convention.

3] The bid of a new suit by opener guarantees at least a good five-card suit, and is forcing.

4] Game must be reached if a satisfactory suit fit is found, so any bid below game after a trump suit is agreed upon is forcing.

5] If opener has a good five-card or longer suit *and* a four-card major suit, he may choose to bid his suit rather than use Stayman. Responder should help out by raising with a fit for opener's suit, and otherwise showing a four-card major if he has one.

Let's look at a few examples from responder's side of the table. Suppose that partner has opened 1 ♣, you have responded 1 NT, and opener has made the rebid shown. What call do you make with each of the hands shown below?

Opener's Rebid

1] 2 ♣ ♠ K 10 8 6 ♡ 7 2 ◇ A J 3 ♣ J 10 4 2: Bid 2 ♠. Partner's rebid is the Stayman convention, asking you to show a four-card major suit if you have one and to bid 2 ◇ otherwise.

2] 2 ♡ ♠ K 10 8 6 ♡ Q 7 4 ◇ A 8 6 3 ♣ 9 7: Bid 3 ♡. Raise opener's suit with three-card or longer support. Since a good trump suit has been found, game must be reached and your 3 ♡ bid is forcing. Change a small heart to a small club and you would bid 2 ♠, denying three-card or longer heart support and showing your four-card major on the way back to notrump in case partner has four spades along with his good hearts.

3] 2 NT ♠ 9 8 3 ♡ Q 8 2 ◇ Q J 7 5 ♣ K 10 3: Pass. You have an absolute minimum.

Auctions After Positive 2 NT and 3 NT Responses

Bidding after higher-level notrump responses is also relatively straightforward. When deciding upon a rebid, opener should keep the point ranges shown by each response firmly in mind (11–13 points for the 2 NT response, 14–15 points for the 3 NT response). Since the partnership must have at least 27 points, game will always be reached after these responses.

After a positive 2 NT response, the rebid of a new suit by opener is forcing and shows a good five-card or longer suit; notrump raises are natural; and a 3 ♣ rebid is Stayman. For example, if you open 1 ♣ and partner responds 2 NT, sign off in 3 NT with either

♠ K J 8
♡ K Q 6
◇ A 8 6 4
♣ K 10 2

or

♠ K J 8
♡ K Q 6
◇ A Q 8 6
♣ K 10 2

Bid 3 ♣ (Stayman) with

♠ K J 8 7
♡ K 7
◇ A J 10 4
♣ A 10 7

planning to raise a 3 ♠ response to 4 ♠ and bid 3 NT otherwise. Bid 3 ♡ with

♠ 6
♡ A Q 10 8 7
◇ A Q 10 6
♣ A J 7

After a positive 3 NT response, the rebid of a new suit is still natural and shows a good five-card or longer suit; notrump raises are still natural. However, there is one important change in the procedures. Since responder has 14–15 points and opener has at least 16, slam is very likely, particularly if a suit fit can be found that will convert short suits into additional assets. At the *slam* level, major suits have no great superiority over minor suits, as both require 12 tricks for success. Therefore, after a positive 3 NT response, a 4 ♣ rebid is a *modified* form of Stayman which asks responder to bid *any* four-card suit, starting with his cheapest one. A bid of notrump at any stage is natural and says that the bidder has run out of four-card suits to show. Here's how this works:

Opener	Responder
♠ K 7	♠ A Q J
♡ A J 5 4	♡ 6 3
◇ K 7 3	◇ A 10 8 2
♣ A Q 10 3	♣ K J 9 2

The bidding:

Opener	Responder
1 ♣	3 NT
4 ♣[1]	4 ◇[2]
4 ♡[3]	5 ♣[4]
6 ♣[5]	Pass

[1] "Slam looks likely if we can find a suit fit. How are you fixed for four-card suits?"

[2] "I've got four respectable diamonds."

[3] "Sorry, I don't have four-card or longer support. But I do have four decent hearts."

[4] "No heart support here. I do have four clubs."
(Change a small club to a small heart and responder would bid 4 NT, indicating that he had no more four-card suits. Opener, with only 17 high-card points opposite a maximum of 15, would pass.)

[5] "Good! We've found our slam."

The club slam is made easily by ruffing two small hearts; a notrump slam would have almost no chance. Since the "modified Stayman" 4 ♣ rebid can produce such sizable windfalls, it is well worth your attention. With this valuable weapon added to your bidding arsenal, you should find auctions after a positive notrump response an enjoyable and profitable route to the best contract.

Positive suit responses

A positive suit response (1 ♡, 1 ♠, 2 ♣, or 2 ◊) to your 1 ♣ opening bid shows a five-card or longer suit and 8 or more points. Since partner's hand is relatively unlimited, you will probably need to explore fairly thoroughly in order to determine the best contract, and Precision offers a useful array of bidding weaponry to help you in your quest for lucrative games and slams.

Jump shift rebids by opener

After a 1 ♣ opening bid and a positive suit response, it is usually best to keep the bidding low and allow ample room for exploration. Therefore, jump rebids by opener are used to convey specific messages, and the single jump in a new suit shows a *solid six-card or longer suit and 19 or more points.* This enables you to force to game, designate the trump suit, and suggest the possibility of slam in a single action. For example, if you open 1 ♣ and partner responds 1 ♡, a minimum jump to 2 ♠ is

♠ A K Q J 7 4
♡ 6
◊ A K 3
♣ Q 8 3

Since partner's support may be dismal, you need at least the A K Q 10 in your long suit to make a jump rebid.

After the jump rebid, responder shows minimal values by either bidding notrump as cheaply as possible or making a single raise of your long suit. (If he passes, dismiss him from the table in disgrace, for your jump shift is forcing to game.) With extra strength, responder should cue-bid a new suit.*

---

* It is optional whether this cue-bid should guarantee the ace or simply show a useful feature (such as K Q 2).

For example, suppose that partner opens with 1 ♣, you respond 1 ♡, and partner jumps to 2 ♠. What call would you make with each of the following hands?

> ♠ 6 2 ♡ K J 8 7 5 ◊ J 10 7 4 ♣ K J:
>
> *Bid* 2 NT. You have a minimum positive response, strength in both unbid suits, and a relatively balanced hand.

> ♠ 6 2 ♡ A K J 7 4 ◊ 9 5 4 2 ♣ 6 4:
>
> *Raise to* 3 ♠. Your weak holdings in the unbid suits don't inspire confidence in a notrump contract, and you don't need good spade support because partner has promised a self-sufficient suit.

> ♠ 6 2 ♡ K Q 9 7 4 ◊ 6 4 2 ♣ A K 6:
>
> *Bid* 3 ♣. Cue-bid to show a good hand with excellent values in clubs. If partner makes a minimal rebid (such as 3 ♠), bid 4 ♣ to strongly invite slam.

The 3 NT rebid by opener

If you use up a huge amount of bidding room with your rebid, the implication is that you are not at all interested in exploration. For example, suppose you hold

$$
\begin{array}{l}
\spadesuit \text{ K J 3} \\
\heartsuit \text{ A J 7} \\
\diamondsuit \text{ K Q J 7} \\
\clubsuit \text{ Q 10 3}
\end{array}
$$

You open with 1 ♣, and partner makes a positive 2 ♣ response. You have a balanced minimum with nothing of interest to reveal—no good suit of your own, no four-card major suit, and no interesting and unusual distribution. The best way to convey this message is to jump to 3 NT, strongly suggesting that partner cease and desist. The 3 NT rebid shows 16–18 points, a balanced hand, and stoppers in all unbid suits; it denies a good five-card or longer suit or a four-card major suit.

If responder bids a new suit at the four-level after your 3 NT rebid, he is showing at least 5–5 distribution and is asking you to choose a game contract in one of his two suits. For example, suppose the auction proceeds as follows:

Opener (you)	Responder
1 ♣	1 ♠
3 NT	4 ♡

Responder can't be looking for a 4–4 heart fit because your 3 NT rebid denies a four-card major, so he must have at least five cards in each major. Therefore, you should pass with a doubleton spade and three hearts and return to 4 ♠ with three spades and two or three hearts. If you have a doubleton in both majors, you have made an error! You should rebid 3 NT only with balanced suit distribution (4-3-3-3 or 4-4-3-2, or perhaps 5-3-3-2 with a weak five-card minor). Thus, partner will know that at least one of his five-card suits is assured of satisfactory support, and he can bid 4 ♡ with confidence that he is improving the contract.

If responder's bid over 3 NT is 4 ♣ or 4 ♢, *don't* pass and leave him to languish in a part score; bid game in one of his suits. If you have three-card or longer support for both suits and have the luxury of a choice, prefer a major-suit game to a minor-suit game; otherwise, prefer partner's first suit unless your support for his second suit is longer. Also, responder is expected to use good judgment and pass 3 NT rather than risk reaching five of a minor with a weak 5–5 hand such as

> ♠ K J 4 3 2
> ♡ 6
> ♢ 7 2
> ♣ A J 6 5 3

If responder has a big hand and envisions slam in spite of your minimum, he will probably have enough information after your highly limited 3 NT rebid to bid it directly.

Simple suit rebids by opener

After a 1 ♣ opening bid and a positive suit response, you should bid a *five*-card or longer suit if you have one. As usual, select the higher-ranking suit in case of ties. This rebid is *forcing* and will lead to game unless a misfit is detected. (With misfits, it is usually a good idea to end the auction as soon as possible and get on to the next hand before it occurs to the opponents to make a penalty double.)

For example, suppose the auction has proceeded 1 ♣—1 ♡, and you are opener in quest of a rebid with each of the following hands:

♠ A K 8 7 6   ♡ 7   ◇ A Q 6 3   ♣ K J 2:
Bid 1 ♠.

♠ A Q 8 7 5   ♡ 7   ◇ A Q 10 6 4 3   ♣ A:
Bid 2 ◇. You will bid and rebid spades to show your 6–5 distribution.

♠ A Q J 7 5   ♡ K J 7   ◇ A Q 2   ♣ 7 3:
Bid 1 ♠. You know that hearts will be a good trump suit because partner has at least five and you have three, but first clarify your distribution by showing your spade suit. You will support hearts next time.

♠ K 8 6 3   ♡ ——   ◇ K J 7 2   ♣ A K Q 10 2:
Bid 2 ♣.

Now let's move across the table and suppose that partner has opened 1 ♣, you have made a positive suit response, and partner has bid a new suit. Your first step is to determine whether your positive response is *minimum* or *above-minimum*, using the following evaluation procedures:

Above-minimum positive response: 11 or more points *and* one of the following: 1] at least two aces, *or* 2] one ace and at least two kings, *or* 3] four kings.

Minimum positive response: Any 8–10 point hand, and any hand with 11 or more points which lacks the requisite number of aces and kings.

The reason for specifying aces and kings as well as points is that slam is likely if you have an above-minimum positive response, but a high-level contract will prove notably unsuccessful if many of the partnership points are located in queens and jacks and the opponents can cash enough top tricks to defeat the contract even before you get started. A scheme which may help you to remember these rules is to count each ace as "2 controls" and each king as "1 control." Then,

> *Above-minimum positive response* = 11 or more points *and* at least 4 controls;

> *Minimum positive response* = Any 8–10 point hand or any hand with 0–3 controls.

Some examples are shown below. In each case, partner has opened the bidding with 1 ♣, you have responded 1 ♠, and partner has rebid 2 ♡.

♠ A 7 5 4 3   ♡ 6 5   ♢ A 6 3   ♣ 9 3 2:   Minimum.
(8 points)

♠ A 7 5 4 3   ♡ K 5   ♢ K 6 3   ♣ 8 4 2:   Minimum.
(10 points)

♠ Q J 7 3 2   ♡ J 3   ♢ A Q 2   ♣ Q 10 3:   Minimum.
(You have 12 points but only 2 controls. A positive response with only one ace must have at least two kings to be above minimum.)

♠ K J 8 7 4   ♡ K 3   ♢ K 10 2   ♣ J 3 2:   Minimum.
(You have 11 points but only 3 controls. A positive response with no aces at all must have all four kings to be above minimum.)

♠ A 10 7 6 4   ♡ 6 5   ♢ A Q 5   ♣ J 10 3:   Above minimum.   (11 points and 4 controls.)

♠ A K 7 3 2   ♡ 5 2   ♢ K 4 3   ♣ J 10 3:   Above minimum.   (11 points and 4 controls.)

♠ A K 7 3 2   ♡ K 7 4 2   ◊ 6 5 3   ♣ 2:   Above
minimum. (Since you certainly plan to raise hearts
with such fine support, you count 3 points for the
singleton club and have 13 points and 4 controls.)

♠ A K J 7 6   ♡ A 7   ◊ K 8 3   ♣ Q 4 2:   Above
minimum. (17 points and 6 controls; there is no
upper limit to "above minimum.")

If you have a *minimum* positive response, let partner know
by taking one of the following actions, all of which are forcing
for at least one round:

*Make a single raise of opener's suit with three-card or
longer support.* Even a minimum positive response
should offer a good play for game opposite a 1 ♣
opening if a satisfactory suit fit is located, so this raise
is forcing to game. Opener will sign off in game
unless he sees a chance for slam in spite of your
minimum, in which case he will cue-bid a new suit.

Bid notrump as cheaply as possible. This shows a
relatively balanced minimum with poor support for
opener's suit.

Bid a new suit of four or more cards. But *don't* bid very
weak suits if a reasonable alternative can be found.

Rebid a six-card or longer suit. Your first response has
already shown a five-card suit, so don't rebid it unless
it is longer than originally advertised. It is better to
rebid a six-card or longer *major* than to raise opener's
minor or bid a new four-card minor, because game in
a major requires one trick less than game in a minor.

If you are fortunate enough to hold an *above-minimum*
positive response, the rebidding procedures are similar except
that you *jump* the bidding to let partner in on the good news.
That is, you jump raise opener's suit with three-card or longer

support, jump in notrump with a relatively balanced hand and poor support for opener's suit; jump rebid your own six-card or longer suit; or jump in a *good* new suit of four or more cards (at least as strong as K Q 3 2) provided that you do not pass the 3 NT level with a relatively balanced hand. All these jumps are forcing to game and invite slam.

Some examples:

Opener	Responder (you)
1 ♣	1 ♠
2 ♡	?

♠ K 10 8 5 3   ♡ 9 7 4   ◊ A J 6 2   ♣ 7:
Bid 3 ♡. You have 11 points in support of hearts but only 3 controls, so your positive response is minimum. Your raise is forcing to game because a good suit fit has been detected, and it will convey much more information than would bidding diamonds.

♠ K 10 8 5 3   ♡ 7 4   ◊ A J 6 2   ♣ 9 7:
Bid 3 ◊. Since you lack heart support, show your respectable diamond suit. A 3 ♠ bid by opener is forcing to game because a good fit has been found, so continue on to 4 ♠. Pass a 3 NT rebid.

♠ K 10 8 5 3   ♡ 7 4   ◊ K Q 2   ♣ 7 4 3:
Bid 2 NT, showing a relatively balanced minimum positive response with poor heart support. A 3 ♣ rebid by opener is forcing, and you should bid 3 NT because you have the unbid suit stopped. However, *don't* bid 3 NT over a 3 ◊ rebid; you don't have the unbid club suit stopped. (Recommended choice: 3 ♡.) Raise a 3 ♠ rebid to 4 ♠; pass a 3 NT rebid.

♠ Q J 7 3 2   ♡ J 3   ◊ A Q 2   ♣ Q 10 3:
Bid 2 NT. This is forcing for one round, so you still have time to make sure that game is reached. If

opener now bids 3 ♣, 3 ◊, or 3 ♡, you will bid
3 NT. Don't let your queens and jacks delude you
into thinking that you have an above-minimum
response!

♠ A Q 8 6 5 3　♡ ——　◊ K 10 4 3　♣ 7 3 2:
Bid 2 ♠. Prefer rebidding a six-card major to bidding
a new four-card minor. Opener will now know that
doubleton support for your suit is sufficient. If he
rebids 3 ♡, his spade support must be about as bad as
your heart support and a dangerous misfit exists,
so pass and hope that nobody doubles.*

♠ A K 7 3 2　♡ J 4 3　◊ K Q 5 3　♣ 4:
Jump to 4 ♡ to show an above-minimum positive
response with at least three-card heart support.
Supporting partner's major suit is the most
informative rebid that you can make.

♠ A K 7 3 2　♡ 5 2　◊ K 4 3　♣ J 10 3:
Jump to 3 NT, showing a relatively balanced
above-minimum positive response with poor heart
support.

♠ A Q J 6 5　♡ 10 7　◊ A Q 7 3　♣ 7 5:
Jump to 3 NT. Your diamond suit is strong enough
for a jump to 4 ◊, but it is a poor idea to pass the
3 NT level with a relatively balanced hand. Partner is
permitted to pass your 3 NT bid with a balanced
minimum, and you will surely be in the best contract
if he does so.

♠ A Q J 6 5　♡ ——　◊ A Q 7 3　♣ J 6 4 2:
Jump to 4 ◊, showing an above-minimum positive

---

* If someone does double and a disaster ensues, you may find some com-
fort in the thought that standard bidding, which would begin 1 ♡—1 ♠—
3 ♡, would do no better and might easily do even worse.

response which lacks heart support, has at least four good diamonds, and is not suitable for notrump play. Ignore the abysmal clubs.

♠ A K 7 3 2   ♡ 6 2   ◇ A K J 3   ♣ A 2:
Almost any rebid would probably work with this awesome collection! The point of this example is *not* to rebid 3 NT, which partner can pass with a balanced minimum. (Recommended choice: 4 ◇.)

♠ A J 9 8 6 3   ♡ 5   ◇ A Q 7 3   ♣ 10 7:
Jump to 3 ♠.

After a *minimum* rebid by responder, any bid below game is forcing *if* a satisfactory trump suit has been found. If not, a new-suit bid by opener is forcing, but a simple rebid of his own suit can and should be passed if responder has only 8 or a bad 9 points. If opener goes directly to an appropriate game contract, his bid is an absolute signoff.

After a *jump* rebid by responder, game must be reached, and opener may pass only if the jump rebid is 3 NT. Otherwise, he should flash a warning signal with minimal values by making a discouraging rebid, such as the cheapest possible bid in his own suit or a suit bid by responder. With extra strength, opener should cue-bid a new suit or jump in his own suit to show a solid suit of at least six cards. For example:

A	Opener	Responder	B	Opener	Responder
	1 ♣	1 ♡		1 ♣	1 ♠
	1 ♠	3 ◇		2 ♡	4 ♣
	4 ♠			4 ◇	

In example A, responder's jump to 3 ◇ promises an above-minimum positive response, and opener's jump to 4 ♠ shows extra values and a solid suit. Since everyone in sight is bristling with extra strength except the unfortunate opponents, responder is expected to bid again and should usually cue-bid a side-suit value now that spades is the agreed-upon trump suit

In example B, however, a non-jump rebid of 4 ♠ over

responder's 4 ♣ bid would show a minimum 1 ♣ opening. Therefore, opener has decided to bid 4 ◇ to show extra strength (and a valuable feature in diamonds).

In both examples, a bid of game by opener in responder's suit is always a signoff and denies any further interest in slam.

The simple NT rebid by opener

If you (opener) don't happen to have a good suit of your own and your hand doesn't qualify for a 3 NT rebid, your choice of rebid will depend upon whether or not you have good support for responder's suit. When your support is *poor* (0–2 cards), you should bid notrump as cheaply as possible. This rebid is *forcing*, relatively *un*limited, and denies possession of a five-card or longer suit (except for a weak five card *minor* that is too pathetic to mention).

For example, after the auction 1 ♣—1 ♡, rebid 1 NT with each of the following hands:

♠ K Q 8 3　♡ 7 2　◇ A J 6 3　♣ A Q 3
(Don't rebid 3 NT with a four-card major.)

♠ K J　♡ K 2　◇ A K Q 7　♣ J 9 6 4 3
(Don't rebid 3 NT with unbalanced suit distribution. The clubs are too weak to bother with.)

♠ K Q 8　♡ 7 6　◇ A K Q 9　♣ A J 10 3
(Don't rebid 3 NT with more than 18 points.)

Similarly, after the auction 1 ♣—2 ◇, rebid 2 NT with

♠ K Q 8 7　♡ K Q 6 2　◇ 10 8　♣ A Q 10

or

♠ A K J　♡ A K 9 7　◇ 6 4　♣ K Q 9 5

Now let's see how matters look from responder's viewpoint. If partner has opened with 1 ♣ and made a simple notrump

If the fates have been kind and you hold an *above-minimum* positive response, proceed similarly but *jump* the bidding to convey the glad tidings to partner. That is, jump in a *good* new four-card or longer suit, jump rebid a six-card or longer suit, or jump in notrump.* All of these jump rebids are forcing for at least one round, ensure that game will be reached, and are invitational to slam.

To illustrate these procedures, let's suppose that the auction has gone as follows:

Opener	Responder (you)
1 ♣	1 ♡
1 NT	?

Note that there is no possibility of counting distribution points at this stage because there is no suit for you to raise. As responder, what call would you make with each of the following hands?

♠ 10 6   ♡ K J 8 7 5   ◇ 6 4 3   ♣ A 6 2:
Bid 2 ♣, showing exactly 8 points and denying a four-card or longer spade or diamond suit. Partner is requested to name the final contract on his next turn.

♠ 10 6   ♡ K J 8 7 5   ◇ A 9 3 2   ♣ 5 4:
Bid 2 ◇. If opener rebids 2 NT, showing a 16-point minimum, pass because you have only 8 points. If instead opener raises to 3 ◇, you must bid again because a good suit fit has been found. With such meager values, try for the nine-trick game by bidding 3 NT.

* With an *above-minimum* positive response, there is no need for a special warning signal, so the club suit is *not* treated differently from any other suit.

rebid over your positive suit response, first decide whether you have a *minimum* or an *above-minimum* positive response. Recall that

> Above-minimum positive response = 11 or more points *and* at least 4 controls;
>
> Minimum positive response = Any 8–10 point hand or any hand with 0–3 controls.

If you have ascertained that you have a *minimum* positive response, proceed as follows:

> *Bid clubs as cheaply as possible with exactly 8 points and no unbid four-card suit.* (You may have four *clubs*.) This bid is *not* forcing. If partner has a 16-point minimum, he will cleverly deduce that your side has only 24 points and will therefore stop short of game. Whatever partner's holding, he is expected to name the final contract on his next turn.
>
> *Bid a new four-card or longer diamond, heart, or spade suit.* This bid is forcing for one round. Opener may have one or two four-card major suits, so it is up to you to help locate a 4–4 major fit.
>
> *Rebid a six-card or longer suit.* This bid is also forcing for one round. Prefer rebidding a six-card *major* to introducing a new four-card *minor*; help partner envision a major-suit game with doubleton support for your suit.
>
> *Raise to 2 NT.* This shows at least 9 points and is forcing to game. Be sure to bid 2 NT with 9 or more points and a four-card club suit; a club bid would show exactly 8 points and might well result in a missed game (and an unhappy partner). However,

♠ Q J 7 6   ♡ A Q J 6 2   ◇ J 3 2   ♣ 7:

Bid 2 ♠. You have 11 points but only 2 controls, so do not jump. You should raise a 2 NT rebid to 3 NT, pass if opener signs off by jumping directly to game, and go on to 4 ♠ if opener makes a forcing raise to 3 ♠.

♠ 7 3   ♡ K J 7 6 3   ◇ A Q 5   ♣ 8 6 3:

Bid 2 NT, showing at least 9 points and denying a four-card or longer spade or diamond suit. Opener will probably sign off in 3 NT. (If instead he bids a new suit, he is trying for slam. You have a near-maximum in points and controls and should therefore cue-bid in diamonds.)

♠ 8 3   ♡ K J 7 6 3   ◇ 6 3   ♣ A J 10 4:

Bid 2 NT. A 2 ♣ rebid would show exactly 8 points.

♠ 7 3 2   ♡ A J 10 9 3   ◇ K 10 9   ♣ 7 2:

Bid 2 NT. Your good heart suit and top-card values are just enough of an excuse to take the aggressive action and avoid the 2 ♣ rebid on a doubleton.

♠ K 8 2   ♡ Q J 7 4 2   ◇ Q 8 5   ♣ 10 7:

Bid 2 ♣. This time, there is no good alternative; 2 NT might well get you to a hopeless game.

♠ 5 4   ♡ A Q 7 5 4 2   ◇ K J 6 3   ♣ 6:

Bid 2 ♡. A six-card major offers a more probable route to game than a four-card minor, so let partner know that doubleton support for your suit is sufficient.

♠ 7   ♡ K J 8 7 4   ◇ A K 6 3   ♣ 6 4 2:

Jump to 3 ◇ to show an above-minimum positive response with a good four-card diamond suit.

♠ A 3   ♡ Q 9 7 6 2   ◇ A J 8   ♣ K 6 3:
Jump to 3 NT (forcing).

♠ 6   ♡ A K J 6 5 3   ◇ A 6 2   ♣ 7 4 2:
Jump to 3 ♡.

After a minimum club rebid by responder, opener should name the final contract on his next turn, and he may pass if he has only 16 high-card points with five clubs. After any other minimum rebid, opener must bid again, and the auction proceeds naturally. Responder has the option of stopping short of game if opener makes a minimal rebid (such as 2 NT), but game must be reached if a good suit fit is found. Any game bid by opener is a signoff.

If responder has shown an above-minimum positive response by jumping the bidding, game must be reached. With a minimum, opener should flash the caution sign by bidding notrump or choosing a trump suit as cheaply as possible. With extra strength, opener should cue-bid a new suit.

Raises of responder's suit by opener

If you (opener) don't have a good suit of your own and have *good* support (3 or more cards) for responder's suit, let him know that a good fit has been found by taking one of the following actions, all of which are *forcing to game:*

Raise a major suit to the four-level with a 16-point minimum. As usual, using up large amounts of bidding room indicates an extreme lack of interest in exploration, and partner will pass unless he has a superb hand which offers a good chance for slam.

Jump raise with 19–21 points. If responder sees no chance for slam, he simply signs off by going on to game; with enough extra strength to envision slam, he cue-bids a new suit.

> *Rebid 1 NT and then support responder's suit with 17–18 points.* Responder will sign off in game if slam is out of the question and will cue-bid if he would like additional information. The reason for not making a direct single raise is that this bid has a special meaning in Precision, as we will see in the next section.

Be sure to cast the usual suspicious eye at *minor*-suit fits; strongly consider playing in 3 NT instead if your hand is relatively balanced. Also, remember to count your distribution points in all of these cases because you are raising partner's suit. Some examples:

	Opener (you)	Responder
	1 ♣	1 ♠
	?	

♠ K 6 3   ♡ A Q 6   ◇ A K 4 3   ♣ 8 3 2:
> *Bid 4 ♠.* You are totally uninterested in prolonging the issue with your 16-point balanced minimum, and the unstopped clubs could be ruinous in a notrump contract.

♠ Q 7 6 3   ♡ A 10 6 2   ◇ A K 9 7   ♣ A:
> *Bid 3 ♠.* Counting 3 points for the club singleton when raising partner's suit, your hand is worth 20 points. Partner will sign off in 4 ♠ with a minimum and cue-bid if he sees a chance for slam.

♠ Q 7 6 3   ♡ K 10 7 2   ◇ A K 10   ♣ A 7:
> *Bid 1 NT.* You will bid spades next time to show 17–18 points and at least three-card spade support.

On some occasions, you may hold 22 or more points and very good support for partner's suit. Most such hands will find an ideal solution in the *trump asking bid,* which will be discussed in the next section.

PRECISION SYSTEM

The trump asking bid by opener

In Precision, the *single raise of responder's suit* after a 1 ♣ opening bid and a positive suit response *agrees upon responder's suit as the trump suit and asks him how good his suit is.* For example:

A	Opener	Responder
	1 ♣	1 ♡
	2 ♡ (trump asking bid)	

B	Opener	Responder
	1 ♣	2 ◇
	3 ◇ (trump asking bid)	

This special convention can reap a huge profit. A sketchy trump suit will mean disaster in a high-level contract, but it is too late to do anything about it after the dummy comes down; so Precision enables you to find out exactly how good the combined trump suit is at a low level of bidding.

Responder's answer to the asking bid is in terms of bidding *"steps."* In auction A, for example, a 2 ♠ rebid by responder is *one step* above the previous bid of 2 ♡; a 2 NT rebid is *two steps* above 2 ♡; a 3 ♣ rebid represents *three steps* upward; and so on. In auction B, a 3 ♡ rebid by responder is *one step* above the last bid of 3 ◇; a 3 ♠ bid represents *two steps;* a 3 NT bid represents *three steps;* and so on. Here's what the steps mean:

Steps	Suit Length	Number of Top Honors (A, K, or Q)
1	5 or more cards	0
2	5 cards	1
3	5 cards	2
4	6 or more cards	1
5	6 or more cards	2
6	5 or more cards	3

To see how this works in practice, suppose you open 1 ♣ holding

> ♠ K 6 5 3 2
> ♡ A K Q J 10
> ◇ A 6
> ♣ A

You plan to show both of your major suits over the expected negative response, but partner surprises you by bidding 1 ♠. Raise to 2 ♠ (the *trump asking bid*) and then proceed as follows:

Responder's answer	*Your action*
2 NT *(1 step)*	Sign off in 4 ♠. The highest spade partner can have is the jack.
3 ♣ *(2 steps)*	Bid 6 ♠. Partner has either five spades to the ace or five spades to the queen. If he has the queen, your chances of avoiding two trump losers (and making slam) are excellent; if he has the ace, the chances of not losing any trump tricks are not good enough to warrant a grand slam.
3 ◇ *(3 steps)*	Bid a grand slam. Partner has five spades to the A Q. You should use Blackwood to check for kings (first bid 4 NT, then 5 NT) and bid 7 NT if partner has a king. If he has no kings, bid 7 ♠ and score the thirteenth trick via a club ruff.
3 ♡ *(4 steps)*	Bid 4 NT (Blackwood). Partner has six or more spades to the ace *or* queen. If the former is true, the

Responder's answer	*Your action*
	enemy spades must fall in two rounds and you will bid 7 NT. If instead partner has the queen, play in 6 ♠.
3 ♠ *(5 steps)*	Bid 7 NT. Partner has six or more spades to the A Q and you can count 13 top tricks.
3 NT *(6 steps)*	Call for a new deck. Partner is showing the A K Q, but you have the king.
Pass	Do something drastic (like throw your cards out the window). Don't continue playing with a partner who passes an asking bid!

Note how the trump asking bid helps you determine vital strength and length. It also keeps the opponents completely in the dark as to your hand. (A diamond lead *might* beat 6 ♠ if you are off the spade ace, but the opponents have no clue and may easily lead a club—or even a heart.)

After a trump asking bid, it is also possible to inquire about responder's holding in an important side suit. These subsequent asking bids will be presented in Chapter 12.

When the opponents interfere

If the 1 ♣ opening bid is followed by a takeout double, positive notrump and suit responses retain the standard meaning and the procedures described in this chapter are fully applicable. If the 1 ♣ opening is followed by an overcall, however, the meanings of responder's first bid change dramatically. (See Chapter 2.) For example, a notrump response is unlimited and forcing and shows an unbalanced hand, while a simple new suit bid shows a five-card suit and 5–8 points. If responder has made an unlimited forcing bid, describe your hand as best you can by bidding a five-card or longer suit, bidding notrump with at least one stopper in the enemy suit and no good suit of your own, or cue-bidding the enemy suit. If responder's hand is limited, you should have a good idea as to the best contract and can explore further if necessary by bidding a new suit below the level of game (forcing) or cue-bidding the enemy suit.

Bidding after a 1♣ opening and a positive response

1] Positive NT responses

Response	Opener's Rebid
1 NT	2 ♣ = Stayman. 2 ◇, 2 ♡, or 2 ♠ = forcing, good five-card or longer suit. 2 NT = non-forcing, invitational to 3 NT. 3 NT = signoff. 4 NT = non-forcing, invitational to 6 NT.
2 NT	Similar to rebid after 1 NT response. (In particular, note that 3 ♣ = Stayman.)
3 NT	Similar to rebid after lower-level notrump responses except that 4 ♣ = *modified* Stayman asking for *any* four-card suit.

2] Positive suit responses (1♥, 1♠, 2♣, 2♦)

Opener's Rebid

Simple suit rebid =
at least *five*
cards in bid
suit; relatively
unlimited; forcing.

Responder's Rebid

1. Determine whether positive suit response is:

   ABOVE-MINIMUM: 11 points *and* 4 or more *controls* (ace = 2 controls, king = 1 control).

   MINIMUM: Any 8–10 point hand or any hand with 0–3 controls.

2. Bids with MINIMUM positive response (all forcing):

   Single raise of opener's suit with three-card or longer support.

   New four-card or longer suit.

Opener's Rebid	Responder's Rebid
	Denies support for opener's suit. Prefer a simple notrump bid if suit is very weak.
	Simple notrump bid. Denies support for opener's suit or a good new suit.
	Rebid a six-card or longer suit. Prefer rebidding a six-card *major* to bidding or raising a minor suit.
	3. Bids with ABOVE-MINIMUM positive response (all forcing to *game*): Similar to minimum bids, but *jump* the bidding. (However, don't pass the 3 NT level with a relatively balanced hand.)
Simple notrump rebid = no five-card or longer suit (except perhaps for a weak five-card minor); relatively unlimited; forcing.	1. Determine whether positive suit response is ABOVE-MINIMUM or MINIMUM.
	2. Bids with MINIMUM positive response:
	Simple club bid = exactly 8 points, no unbid four-card or longer suit. *Not* forcing.
	New four-card or longer suit (other than clubs). Forcing. Prefer a single notrump raise if suit is very weak.
	Rebid a six-card or longer suit. Forcing. Prefer rebidding a six-card *major* to bidding a four-card minor.
	Single notrump raise = 9 or more points, forcing to game.

PRECISION SYSTEM

Opener's Rebid	Responder's Rebid

3. Bids with ABOVE-MINIMUM positive response (all forcing to *game*): Similar to minimum bids, but *jump* the bidding. (Club bids are *not* special. Don't pass the 3 NT level with a relatively balanced hand.)

Single raise =
trump asking bid.
Asks responder to
describe his suit.
Forcing to game.

Steps Above Opener's Rebid	Suit Length	Suit Strength
1	5 or more cards	J-high or worse
2	5 cards	A or K or Q
3	5 cards	AK or AQ or KQ
4	6 or more cards	A or K or Q
5	6 or more cards	AK or AQ or KQ
6	5 or more cards	AKQ

Jump raise =
19–21 points,
good support.
Forcing to game.

Game in agreed suit = signoff.
Cue-bid = feature-showing,
slam try.

Jump Shift = *Solid*
six-card or longer
suit and 19 or
more points.
Forcing to game.
(Suit headed by
at least
A K Q 10.)

Single raise = minimal values.
Single notrump = minimal values
with some strength in all unbid
suits.
Cue-bid = extra values and
interest in slam. (Responder
need not worry about support
as opener has promised a
self-sufficient suit.)

3 NT = 16–18 points,
no good five-card
or longer suit or
four-card major; no
void or singleton.

New suit = at least 5–5
distribution, asks opener to
select game in one of
responder's suits.

Opener's Rebid	Responder's Rebid
All unbid suits stopped.	
Jump raise to 4 ♡ or 4 ♠ = 16 points, no good five-card or longer suit, at least three-card support for responder's suit.	*Pass* with little chance for slam; *cue-bid* with excellent hand and good chance for slam.

REVIEW QUIZ

PART I.

You have opened with 1 ♣ and partner has made the positive response shown in each of the following problems. What is your rebid?

1] *Responder's Bid* 1 NT
   ♠ A J 2
   ♡ K 10 3
   ◇ A J 7 5 2
   ♣ A Q

2] *Responder's Bid* 2 ◇
   ♠ K Q 6 3
   ♡ K Q 8
   ◇ 7 4
   ♣ A Q 10 3

3] *Responder's Bid* 1 NT
   ♠ K J 3
   ♡ A Q 8 6 5
   ◇ A K 6
   ♣ 3 2

4] *Responder's Bid* 2 ♣
   ♠ K Q 10 5 3
   ♡ 6
   ◇ A K Q J 5
   ♣ J 7

5] *Responder's Bid* 1 ♠
   ♠ –
   ♡ A K Q 10 8 7 3
   ◇ K 8 3
   ♣ A K J

6] *Responder's Bid* 1 ♡
   ♠ 7 2
   ♡ K J 3
   ◇ A Q 8 7
   ♣ A K 10 4

7] *Responder's Bid* 2 NT
   ♠ K J 7 5
   ♡ 10 8
   ◇ K Q 5
   ♣ A K 4 3

8] *Responder's Bid* 1 ♡
   ♠ A Q J 8 6
   ♡ A 10 3
   ◇ A K 7 3
   ♣ 6

9] *Responder's Bid* 1 Nᵀ
   ♠ K Q 8 6
   ♡ A Q 7 2
   ◇ K 3
   ♣ A 10 3

10] *Responder's Bid* 1 ♠
   ♠ K 10 7
   ♡ K 3
   ◇ A Q 10 5
   ♣ A K 10 7

11] *Responder's Bid* 1 ♠
   ♠ J 4
   ♡ K Q 6
   ◇ A Q 7 5
   ♣ K Q 9 4

12] *Responder's Bid* 1 ♡
   ♠ K Q 7 5
   ♡ 7 4
   ◇ A K 8
   ♣ A Q J 6

13] *Responder's Bid* 1 ♡
   ♠ A 7
   ♡ Q J 6 2
   ◇ A K Q 8 6 4
   ♣ A

PART II.

You are responder and the bidding proceeds as shown in each of the following problems. What is your rebid?

14] Opener Responder
1♣   2◇
2♡   ?
♠ Q82
♡ Q63
◇ AJ10764
♣ 5

15] Opener Responder
1♣   1♡
1 NT   ?
♠ A1076
♡ QJ865
◇ AQ5
♣ 9

16] Opener Responder
1♣   1 NT
2♣   ?
♠ KQ86
♡ J542
◇ K107
♣ 76

17] Opener Responder
1♣   1♡
1 NT   ?
♠ 73
♡ AQ10074
◇ K93
♣ 632

18] Opener Responder
1♣   1 NT
2♠   ?
♠ Q86
♡ K3
◇ K102
♣ J10832

19] Opener Responder
1♣   1♡
1♠   ?
♠ 73
♡ KJ762
◇ KJ87
♣ J6

20] Opener Responder
1♣   1♠
1 NT   ?
♠ QJ765
♡ A93
◇ 63
♣ J105

21] Opener Responder
1♣   1♠
2♠   ?
♠ AJ753
♡ K862
◇ K52
♣ 8

22] Opener Responder
1♣   1 NT
2 NT   ?
♠ K83
♡ 72
◇ J842
♣ A632

23] Opener Responder
1♣   1♡
1 NT   ?
♠ K42
♡ AQJ765
◇ K3
♣ 74

24] Opener Responder
1♣   1♠
2◇   ?
♠ QJ1086
♡ KJ7
◇ J2
♣ J107

25] Opener Responder
1♣   1♡
1♠   ?
♠ 7
♡ AJ965
◇ KJ3
♣ 9432

26] Opener Responder
1♣   1♠
3◇   ?
♠ K9862
♡ AQ3
◇ 76
♣ K106

27] Opener Responder
1♣   1♠
3♠   ?
♠ KQJ75
♡ QJ3
◇ 743
♣ 62

28] Opener Responder
1♣   3 NT
4♣   ?
♠ AQ86
♡ 75
◇ AJ106
♣ K108

29] Opener	Responder
1♣	2♣
2♡	?

♠ A 7 3
♡ 6 2
♢ K 10 3
♣ A Q J 6 5

30] Opener	Responder
1♣	2 NT
3♣	?

♠ K 8 3
♡ Q 6 3
♢ 7 5 3
♣ A K 5 4

31] Opener	Responder
1♣	1♡
3 NT	?

♠ 6 2
♡ Q 9 7 6 3
♢ 7
♣ K Q J 6 2

32] Opener	Responder
1♣	2♢
2 NT	?

♠ K 10 3
♡ 7 2
♢ A J 9 6 3
♣ 8 4 2

33] Opener	Responder
1♣	1♡
2♢	?

♠ J 8 3
♡ A J 8 7 6 2
♢ Q 8 3
♣ 2

34] Opener	Responder
1♣	1♠
1 NT	?

♠ K J 7 6 5
♡ Q J 3
♢ Q
♣ Q J 8 3

35] Opener	Responder
1♣	1♡
1 NT	?

♠ A K 8
♡ A Q J 7 6
♢ K J 7
♣ 7 6

Solutions

1] *Three notrump.* Slam is beyond reach even if partner has a maximum and notrump should be a fine contract, so there is nothing to be gained by bidding diamonds.

2] *Two notrump.* Don't jump to 3 NT with a four-card major; leave room for partner to explore for a 4-4 major suit fit.

3] *Two hearts.* Show a five-card or longer major suit after a positive notrump response.

4] *Two spades.* With two five-card or two six-card suits, first bid the higher-ranking suit. The rebid of a new suit is forcing, so you can bid diamonds next time.

5] *Three hearts.* Jump shift to show a solid six-card or longer suit and 19 or more points.

6] *One notrump.* You will support hearts next time to show 17-18 points and at least three-card support. A direct single raise would be the trump asking bid.

7] *Three clubs.* Use Stayman to investigate a 4-4 spade fit.

8] *One spade.* First show your good five-card suit, and then support hearts next time. A direct jump to 3 ♡ would deny a five-card or longer side suit.

9] *Two clubs.* Use Stayman to search out a 4-4 major suit fit.

10] *Three spades.* Jump raise to show 19-21 points and at least three-card support.

11] *Three notrump.* Strongly suggest to partner that you stop here.

12] *One notrump.* You have poor support for partner's suit and no good five-card or longer suit of your own.

13] *Two hearts.* An ideal situation for the trump asking bid. If partner bids 2 ♠, showing five or more small hearts, sign off in 4 ♡; if he bids 2 NT, showing five hearts to either the ace or king, bid 6 ♡; if he bids 3 ♣, showing five hearts to the ace-king, bid 7 ♡. Similarly, play in 6 ♡ after a 3 ◇ response (showing six or more hearts to one of the top honors) and contract for grand slam after a 3 ♡ response (showing six or more hearts to the ace-king).

14] *Three hearts.* Supporting partner's major is much more informative than rebidding a minor suit. Since a good fit has been found, this raise is forcing to game.

15] *Three spades.* Be sure to jump the bidding with an above-minimum positive response.

16] *Two spades.* Reply to partner's Stayman bid by showing your stronger major. If opener rejects it by returning to no-trump, unveil the heart suit.

17] *Two notrump.* Shows a relatively balanced minimum positive response with at least 9 points.

18] *Three spades.* Shows a minimum positive response with at least three-card spade support.

19] *Two diamonds.* With poor spade support, show your good four-card suit.

20] *Two clubs.* Shows exactly 8 points and no good new suit to bid. Partner is expected to name the contract on his next turn.

21] *Three clubs.* Opener's single raise of your suit is the trump asking bid; move up two steps above the last bid to show a five-card suit headed by one of the top three honors.

22] *Pass.* Not all roads lead to game. You should reject partner's invitation with only 8 points.

23] *Three hearts.* Shows an above-minimum positive response with at least a six-card suit.

24] *Two notrump.* Shows a relatively balanced minimum positive response with poor support for opener's suit.

25] *One notrump.* The pitiful clubs are not worth bidding, and a reasonable alternative exists.

26] *Three hearts.* Partner's jump shift shows a solid suit and designates diamonds as the trump suit. Cue-bid to show a good hand with important values in hearts.

27] *Four spades.* Don't pass! Partner's jump raise shows 19–21 points and is forcing to game; it leaves room for you to cue-bid below game if you have extra strength.

28] *Four diamonds.* After a 3 NT response, a 4 ♣ bid by opener is *modified* Stayman. Start your reply with your lowest-ranking four-card suit.

29] *Three notrump.* This shows an above-minimum positive response with poor support for opener's suit and no good new suit.

30] *Three diamonds.* The negative reply to partner's Stayman bid.

31] *Pass.* Showing your club suit will get you to the five-level if partner can't support hearts, and your hand isn't strong enough to risk this possibility.

32] *Three clubs.* Shows exactly 8 points. Partner will take it from here.

33] *Two hearts.* Prefer rebidding a six-card *major* to supporting opener's *minor*. (After a 1 ♠ rebid, however, you would raise to 2 ♠.)

34] *Two notrump.* A 2 ♣ bid would show exactly 8 points, and you have two few controls for a jump.

35] *Three diamonds.* Partner is allowed to p⸋ss if you bid 3 NT. Since you should be cold for at least a small slam, avoid a calamity by choosing a forcing rebid.

6

The weak Notrump

IF YOU ARE USING standard bidding methods and your partner makes a one-level opening bid, you may need to do some adroit steering in order to avoid the wreckage of a disastrous contract. If you keep the bidding open with a weak hand just in case partner has 21 or 22 points, you risk getting to a hopeless contract; if you pass, you may miss a laydown game. With a good hand, you must decide whether or not to try for the lucrative slam bonus, at the risk of snatching defeat from the jaws of victory by throwing away a cold game.

Precision eliminates such sources of potential misery by limiting *all* opening bids other than 1 ♣ and 2 NT to a maximum of 15 points. Let's begin our discussion of the limited opening bids with one of the most important—the weak notrump.

The 1 NT opening bid

A Precision opening bid of 1 NT shows 13–15 points and balanced suit distribution (4-3-3-3, 4-4-3-2, or 5-3-3-2 with a five-card *minor* suit) . For example, open 1 NT with each of the following hands:

♠ K 10 6	♠ Q 8 7	♠ K 9 7
♡ A Q 6 3	♡ A J 6	♡ K 3 2
◇ 7 2	◇ K 6 3	◇ A 6
♣ K J 6 3	♣ K Q 10 3	♣ K J 10 7 6

However, *don't* open 1 NT with hands such as the following:

♠ Q 8 6   ♥ K J 3   ♦ 6 3 2   ♣ A Q 4 2:
> You have only 12 points. (*Pass.*)

♠ K 10 9 7 6   ♥ A J 3   ♦ K 6 2   ♣ K 2:
> You have a five-card major suit. (*Open* 1 ♠.)

♠ K 8 7 3   ♥ Q 10 7   ♦ 7   ♣ A K J 8 6:
> You have unbalanced suit distribution. (*Open* 2 ♣.)

Responding to the weak NT

Signoffs

If partner opens with a weak notrump and there is no chance that your side holds 25 or more points, sign off by bidding a five-card or longer major suit if you have one. If instead you have a six-card or longer minor suit, end the auction by jumping to *three* of the minor. (As we will see later, a response of 2 ♣ or 2 ♦ is Stayman, not a signoff.) Finally, if your hand doesn't qualify for either of these signoffs, bring matters to a halt by passing. Some examples of these responses after a 1 NT opening bid by partner:

♠ Q 8 3   ♥ 7 2   ♦ A 8 7 6   ♣ Q 6 3 2:
> *Pass.* Your side has at most 23 points, and your hand doesn't qualify for a suit signoff.

♠ Q 8 6 3   ♥ 7 2   ♦ K 8 3   ♣ J 10 6 2:
> *Pass.* A Stayman bid would express interest in game, so you cannot afford to look for a 4–4 spade fit.

♠ 6 2   ♥ 7 4 3   ♦ A Q 8 7 3   ♣ 7 3 2:
> *Pass.* A 2 ♦ response would be Stayman.

♠ A Q 8 7 3   ♥ 7 4 3   ♦ 7 3 2   ♣ 6 2:
> *Bid* 2 ♠. Partner must pass.

♠ 7   ♥ 6 3 2   ♦ K J 10 9 7 6   ♣ 5 4 2:
> *Bid* 3 ♦. Partner must pass.

♠ 8 7 6 4 3   ♡ A J 10 9 8   ◇ 3 2   ♣ 6:
> *Bid 2 ♡*. You don't have time to bid both of your major suits; since they are equal in length, sign off in the stronger one.

NT raises

If you see good game or slam prospects after partner's 1 NT opening bid and you have a balanced hand with no four-card or longer major suit, make an appropriate notrump raise. For example, suppose that partner opens with 1 NT and you hold:

♠ Q 8 3   ♡ K 6 3   ◇ 7 3 2   ♣ A Q 10 6:
> *Raise to* 2 NT. You have 11 points, so you would like to be in game if partner has 14 or 15. The single raise asks him to proceed to 3 NT with a maximum and pass with a minimum.

♠ Q 8 3   ♡ K 7   ◇ Q 10 3 2   ♣ A J 10 6:
> Sign off by jumping to 3 NT. Your side must total at least 25 points, and slam is out of reach.

♠ Q 6 2   ♡ K J 7   ◇ A Q 10   ♣ A K 10 2:
> *Bid* 4 NT. You have 19 points, so your side will total the 33 high-card points needed to bid a small slam in notrump if partner has 14 or 15. The raise to 4 NT is natural, and invites partner to bid 6 NT with a maximum and pass with a minimum.

♠ K 10 3   ♡ K Q 10   ◇ A Q 10   ♣ A Q 7 3:
> Sign off by jumping to 6 NT. Your side must have at least 33 high-card points.

Investigating suit games

With one or two four-card majors, it is usually a good idea to investigate the possibility of a 4–4 major-suit fit by using Stayman. Precision recommends the following procedures:*

---

* Some readers may prefer to use 2 ♣ as the only Stayman bid and treat 2 ◇ as a signoff. If you should select this procedure, be sure you have at least 10 points when you bid 2 ♣.

2 ♣ = *non-forcing* Stayman, invitational to game (8–11 points). Opener bids a four-card major if he has one, choosing 2 ♡ with two four-card majors. With no four-card major, opener bids 2 ◊. Opener should plan on reaching game if he has a maximum, but he should settle for a part score with a minimum.

2 ◊ = *forcing* Stayman; game must be reached (12 or more points). Opener bids a four-card major if he has one, choosing 2 ♡ with two four-card majors. With no four-card major, opener should show a five-card minor if he has one and bid 2 NT otherwise.

For example, if partner has opened the bidding with 1 NT, what call would you make with each of the following hands?

♠ K 8 3 2   ♡ 8 7   ◊ A Q 6   ♣ J 9 3 2:
Bid 2 ♣. You have 10 high-card points and will total 11 points if you can raise spades, so game should be reached if opener has a maximum. Invite game by raising a 2 ♠ rebid to 3 ♠ and bidding 2 NT otherwise.

♠ K 8 3 2   ♡ 8 7   ◊ A Q 6   ♣ K 9 3 2:
Bid 2 ◊. With 12 high-card points, inform partner that game must be reached. If he bids 2 ♠, sign off in 4 ♠; otherwise, sign off in 3 NT.

♠ A Q 8 6 3   ♡ K J 4   ◊ 6 4 3 2   ♣ 7:
Bid 2 ♣. You should invite game with 10 high-card points, and a direct 2 ♠ response would be a signoff. If partner bids 2 ♠, your hand increases in value to 13 points (counting 3 points for the singleton club when raising partner's suit) and you should jump directly to 4 ♠. If partner bids 2 ◊ or 2 ♡, however, just bid 2 ♠, showing a five-card suit (since you are

still interested in spades even though partner doesn't have four-card support) and inviting partner to bid game with a maximum.

♠ A Q 8 6 3   ♡ K J 4 2   ◊ K 6 3   ♣ 5:
Bid 2 ◊. If partner bids 2 ♡ or 2 ♠, sign off raising to game. If he does anything else, bid 3 ♠, offering him a choice between 3 NT and 4 ♠.

Now let's look at these procedures from opener's side of the table:

Opener (you)	Responder
1 NT	2 ♣
?	

♠ Q 9 3 ♡ K Q 6   ◊ 6 3 2   ♣ A Q 10 4:
Bid 2 ◊. You have a minimum and should pass any two-level rebid by responder.

♠ K 8 6 2   ♡ K 3   ◊ 7 3 2   ♣ A K Q 3:
Bid 2 ♠. If partner raises to 3 ♠, go on to 4 ♠; if he bids 2 NT, carry on to 3 NT.

♠ Q J 7   ♡ K 8 3   ◊ K 2   ♣ A J 9 7 6:
Bid 2 ◊. If partner bids 2 ♡ or 2 ♠, showing a five-card suit, your hand is worth 15 points and you should raise to game. If instead responder rebids 2 NT, take the aggressive view with your 14 points and respectable five-card suit and proceed to 3 NT.

If responder's first bid in each of the above examples is 2 ◊, game must be reached. You should bid 2 NT with the first hand, bid 2 ♠ with the second hand, and bid 3 ♣ with the third hand (showing your five-card minor on the way to game in case partner has good club support and visions of slam).

These Stayman bids are very useful. Some hands, however, are handled better by the direct treatment:

♠ A 6 3
♡ A Q 8 7 6
◇ K 4 3 2
♣ 7

If partner opens with 1 NT, you should jump to 3 ♡. This bid is forcing to game and promises at least a five-card heart suit; it asks partner to raise hearts with three-card or longer sup-- port and bid 3 NT with only two-card support. Similarly, a jump response of 3 ♠ is forcing to game and promises at least five spades. If opener has good support and a maximum hand, he should cue-bid en route to game in case responder is interested in slam:

Opener (you)	Responder
1 NT	3 ♡
?	

♠ 6 3   ♡ A 9 7   ◇ K Q 10 7   ♣ A Q 9 6:

Bid 4 ♣. Responder has asked you to choose between 4 ♡ and 3 NT and it would be distinctly unfriendly to disregard his message, so this must be a cue-bid showing at least three-card heart support and a maximum weak notrump. If partner returns to 4 ♡, accept his decision and pass; if instead he cue-bids 4 ◇, bid 5 ◇ to show strength in diamonds and deny values in the bypassed spade suit.

The Gerber convention

After a 1 NT opening bid, a 4 ♣ response is the Gerber ace-asking convention, and opener uses the following replies: 4 ◇ = no aces, 4 ♡ = 1 ace, 4 ♠ = 2 aces, and 4 NT = 3 aces (A weak notrump cannot include four aces.) A 5 ♣ rebid by responder asks for kings (opener replying in a similar fashion) and any other rebid is a signoff.

When the opponents interfere

The responses described in this chapter are almost identical to those used after a Goren 1 NT opening bid. If a weak notrump is followed by a double, however, a change in tactics is

called for. With a weak hand, it is a good idea to try and escape to a suit contract that is less likely to be doubled and penalized. To allow maximum room for maneuvering, 2 ♣ and 2 ♦ responses become signoffs after a double and a redouble shows any good hand (10 or more points).
For example:

Partner	Opponent	You	Opponent
1 NT	Double	?	

♠ 10 7 5 4 3   ♡ 7   ◊ 8 3 2   ♣ Q 9 5 4:
Bid 2 ♠. This is a signoff, just as it would be without the double.

♠ 7   ♡ 6 4 2   ◊ 10 7 5 4 3   ♣ Q 9 5 4:
Bid 2 ◊. After a double, any two-level suit bid is a signoff.

♠ K 8 6 3   ♡ A Q 7 2   ◊ 7 3   ♣ Q 6 2:
Redouble. Partner will pass and leave your right-hand opponent with a most unhappy choice: He can let you play 1 NT redoubled and score a probable bonanza, or he can bid and suffer a probable disaster. If he bids 2 ♡ or 2 ♠, you will double for penalties; if he bids 2 ♣ or 2 ◊, you will pass (forcing) and see if partner wishes to double.

If instead your right-hand opponent competes with an overcall, a double is for penalties; a simple new suit bid is a signoff; a cue-bid of the enemy suit is forcing Stayman; and the jump in a major suit below the level of game is forcing to game and promises at least a five-card suit.

The weak notrump may seem dangerous, but the opponents will usually find it more of a hindrance than a help. When they have the better hands, they must enter the auction with their normal bidding channels totally disrupted (for example, they can no longer open the bidding at the one-level and make the usual responses). To be sure, they may double;

but the partner of the 1 NT bidder has an excellent idea as to opener's strength and distribution and can usually work out a satisfactory course of action. To make matters worse for the beleaguered opponents, 1 NT is the hardest of all contracts to defend against and they are likely to have their work cut out for them if the double is passed out. In the rare cases where a substantial penalty does ensue, the opponents are likely to be cold for game—making the net loss minimal. Finally, with a very weak responding hand (0–4 points), an early ounce of prevention may eliminate the need for a cure:

♠ 8 7 6 3
♡ 10 9 7 3
◊ Q 8 6 5
♣ 2

If partner opens with 1 NT and the next player passes, bid 2 ♣ and pass any rebid that opener makes. Since he is not permitted to rebid 2 NT after non-forcing Stayman, this unusual maneuver is virtually certain to improve the contract and will probably avoid a penalty double by the opponents.

The weak NT

The 1 NT opening bid:
13–15 points, balanced suit distribution (4-3-3-3, 4-4-3-2, or 5-3-3-2 with a five-card *minor* suit).

Responses:
2 ♣ = non-forcing Stayman, invitational to game (8–11 points). Opener bids a four-card major, bids 2 ♡ with two four-card majors, and bids 2 ◊ with no four-card major.

2 ◊ = forcing Stayman; game must be reached (12 or more points). Opener bids a four-card major, choosing 2 ♡ with two four-card majors. With no four-card major, opener shows a five-card minor if he has one and bids 2 NT otherwise.

2 ♡ or 2 ♠ = signoff. Five-card or longer suit.

2 NT = natural, not forcing, 10–11 points. Invitational to 3 NT.

3 ♣ or 3 ◊ = signoff. Six-card or longer suit.

3 ♡ or 3 ♠ = forcing to game, five-card or longer suit. Opener bids 3 NT with only two-card support. With three-card or longer support, opener raises to game with a minimum and cue-bids a new suit with a maximum.

3 NT = signoff.

4 ♣ = Gerber ace asking convention. Opener's replies: 4 ◊ = no aces; 4 ♡ = 1 ace; 4 ♠ = 2 aces; 4 NT = 3 aces.

4 NT = natural, not forcing. Invitational to 6 NT.

Responses after a double:
Any suit bid at the two-level is a signoff; redouble = strong hand (10 or more points).

Responses after an overcall:
Double = penalties; non-jump new suit = signoff; cue-bid = forcing Stayman; jump in major suit below game level = forcing to game, five-card or longer suit.

REVIEW QUIZ

PART I.
What is your opening bid with each of the following hands?

1] ♠ A Q 3	*2]* ♠ A J 8	*3]* ♠ Q J	*4]* ♠ K Q 8 6
♡ K J 2	♡ K Q 10 7 5	♡ Q J 3	♡ A 9 7 2
◊ 8 6	◊ A 10 3	◊ Q J 7 6	◊ K Q 10 5
♣ K 10 7 6 3	♣ 7 2	♣ A Q J 2	♣ 4

PART II.
Partner opens the bidding with 1 NT in each of the following problems. What is your response?

5] ♠ Q 9 8 7 6	*6]* ♠ K 10 8	*7]* ♠ 7
♡ 7	♡ A Q 6	♡ A Q 9 8 6
◊ K 10 8 6 4	◊ Q J 8 6 4	◊ K 6 3
♣ 6 4	♣ K 4	♣ A 10 6 2

8] ♠ K 10 8	*9]* ♠ J 8 6 5	*10]* ♠ K J 7 3
♡ Q J 6	♡ Q 8 3	♡ A Q 9 8 2
◊ Q 9 7 6	◊ A 7	◊ K 5 4
♣ K 8 4	♣ 9 7 6 4	♣ 10

11] ♠ Q 10 8 6	*12]* ♠ 8 2	*13]* ♠ K Q 8
♡ K J 7 4	♡ 9 5 3	♡ A J 7
◊ 7	◊ Q 2	◊ A K 3
♣ A 10 7 6	♣ K Q 10 9 6 3	♣ Q 10 7 3

14] Your right-hand opponent *doubles* and you hold:

♠ 6 3
♡ 7 4 2
◊ 6 3 2
♣ Q 9 8 7 4

15] Your right-hand opponent *overcalls* 2 ♣ and you hold: ♠ K J 8
♡ 7 2
◊ A K 6
♣ 9 8 6 4 2

Solutions

1] *One notrump.* You have 13 points and balanced suit distribution.

2] *One heart.* Don't open 1 NT with a five-card major suit.

3] *One notrump.* With unprotected spade honors and a carload of queens and jacks, only an incurable optimist would value this hand at 16 points.

4] *One diamond.* Don't open 1 NT with unbalanced suit distribution.

5] *Two spades.* The diamonds are a bit stronger, but a 2 ◊ response would be forcing Stayman—not a signoff.

6] *Three notrump.* There is nothing to be gained by bidding diamonds.

7] *Three hearts.* Forcing to game. If partner bids 3 NT, showing a doubleton heart, pass; otherwise, play in 4 ♡.

8] *Two notrump.* Invites partner to continue to 3 NT with a maximum.

9] *Pass.* A Stayman bid would indicate an interest in game, and you are far too weak for such a message.

10] *Two diamonds.* Use forcing Stayman to announce that game must be reached. If partner shows a four-card major suit, raise to game; otherwise, bid 3 ♡ to offer him a choice between 3 NT and 4 ♡.

11] *Two clubs.* If partner bids a major suit, your hand is worth 13 points (counting 3 points for the singleton diamond) and you should raise to game. If he bids 2 ◊, invite game by bidding 2 NT.

12] *Three clubs.* A signoff with a six-card or longer minor suit.

13] *Four notrump.* With 19 points, ask partner to bid 6 NT with a maximum and pass with a minimum.

14] *Two clubs.* After a double, any two-level suit bid is a signoff. (Without the double, you would pass.)

15] *Double.* Your side has at least 24 high-card points, and you have two probable trump tricks and two defensive winners in diamonds. The opponents will certainly not enjoy this result!

7

Auctions
after a 1♥ or 1♠
opening bid

Opening bids of 1 ♥ and 1 ♠

A PRECISION OPENING BID of 1 ♡ or 1 ♠ shows 11–15 points and a five-card or longer suit. (Recall that only high-card points are counted unless you are raising partner's suit.) For example:

♠ A Q 8 6 5　　♡ A J 7 4　　◇ 9 6 3　　♣ 4:
　　Open 1 ♠.

♠ K J 8 6　　♡ Q J 9 7 5　　◇ A K J　　♣ 8:
　　Open 1 ♡.

♠ K J 6 4 3　　♡ A K Q 7 2　　◇ 7　　♣ 10 2:
　　Open 1 ♠. (With two five-card or two six-card suits, bid the nigher-ranking suit.)

However, *don't* open with one of a major with hands such as the following:

♠ A J 8 7 6　　♡ 2　　◇ 3　　♣ A Q 10 7 4 2:
　　You have a longer suit elsewhere. (*Open* 2 ♣)

♠ K 8 6 3　　♡ K 10 8 7　　◇ A Q 6 2　　♣ 3:
　　You don't have a five-card major suit. (*Open* 1 ◇.)

♠ A 7 3　　♡ K Q 10 6 5　　◇ 6 5　　♣ J 9 2:
　　You have only 10 points. (*Pass*.)

Responses to 1♥ and 1♠ opening bids with 0–15 high-card points

If partner opens with a Precision bid of 1 ♡ or 1 ♠, you immediately know a great deal about his hand. One particularly valuable fact at your disposal is that he must have at least five cards in his major suit, so three-card support will be sufficient to produce a good trump suit. Also, you are warned away from overexuberant bidding by the knowledge that opener has a maximum of 15 points.

When responder should pass

One good way of making use of your information about opener's hand is to pass when game is hopelessly out of reach. For example, suppose that partner opens with 1 ♠ and you hold:

♠ 6 2   ♡ K J 9 7 5   ◇ Q 6 3   ♣ 7 3 2:
Pass. There is no possibility of reaching game and no good reason to prolong the issue.

♠ 4   ♡ 8 7 6 2   ◇ Q 7 6 3   ♣ J 4 3 2:
Pass. With this ghastly mess, the best plan is to get on to the next deal as soon as possible.

♠ 8 6   ♡ Q 9 7 2   ◇ K 10 6   ♣ Q 6 5 2:
Pass. You have only 7 points, so game is far out of reach even if opener has a maximum of 15. After the *limited* Precision major-suit opening bid, there is no need to scrape up a response with meager values and poor support for opener's suit.

In sum, you should usually pass a Precision 1 ♡ or 1 ♠ opening bid with an 0–7 point hand and poor support for opener's suit.

Raises by responder

With 8–15 points and good support for opener's major suit, take one of the following actions:

Single raise = 8–10 points, at least three-card support. Not forcing.

Double raise = 11–13 points, at least three-card support. Not forcing.

3 NT = conventional bid showing 14–15 points and at least strong three-card support. Forcing.

Triple raise = Strong preempt based on distributional strength. 14–15 total points with not more than 10 high-card points and at least four-card support. Not forcing.

Remember to count your distribution points when making one of these responses (including 3 NT, which is actually a raise in notrump clothing). Let's look at some examples after a 1 ♡ opening bid by partner:

♠ K 8 4 3   ♡ A 10 5   ◇ 6 3   ♣ 10 9 7 4:
Raise to 2 ♡ with 8 points in support of hearts. Although game is unlikely, the single raise is almost certain to be safe and will make it much harder for the opponents to compete.

♠ 7 3   ♡ Q 8 6   ◇ A Q 10 6   ♣ K 6 3 2:
Raise to 3 ♡ with 12 points in support of hearts.

♠ 7 3   ♡ Q 8 6 2   ◇ A K 7 6   ♣ A 10 4:
Bid 3 NT with 14 points and excellent heart support. Partner will either sign off in 4 ♡ or cue-bid a new suit if he detects a chance for slam.

♠ K J 7 6   ♡ A J 3 2   ◇ 8 7 6 4 2   ♣ ——:
Jump to 4 ♡. An ideal hand for the triple raise.

Precision also recommends the use of *splinter bids—double* jumps in a new suit to show good support for opener's major, 11–15 *high-card* points,* and a *singleton or void* in the bid suit:

♠ 7   ♡ Q 8 6 2   ◊ A K 7 6   ♣ A 10 4 2:
    If partner opens with 1 ♡, respond 3 ♠. This is a splinter bid showing 11–15 high-card points, good heart support, and a singleton or void in spades.

♠ A J 7 6   ♡ Q 8 6 2   ◊ A 10 4 2   ♣ 4:
    If partner opens with 1 ♡ or 1 ♠, respond 4 ♣.

Splinter bids cost virtually nothing to use (when was the last time you responded with a natural 3 ♠ or 4 ♣ bid to partner's 1 ♡ opening?), convey a great deal of information, and sound so startling that they are unlikely to be misunderstood. If you elect to use them, note that the 3 NT response to a 1 ♡ or 1 ♠ opening (equivalent to the forcing double raise in Standard American) will consequently deny any side-suit void or singleton. Also, it is preferable to show a very good five-card or longer suit rather than make a splinter bid.

The splinter bid does much more than help you get to a slam by revealing a singleton or void in the responding hand. It also helps you to stop at game by revealing the duplication of values—too many high cards in the suit shown by the splinter bid—before you have gone past the game level.

After a raise, opener simply determines the combined partnership assets and proceeds accordingly. For example, suppose you open with 1 ♠ holding

♠ A J 8 6 5
♡ K 8 3
◊ K 6 4 2
♣ 5

(11 points). You should pass if partner raises to 2 ♠ or 3 ♠, as your side cannot possibly total the 25 points needed to justify a game bid. If partner bids 3 NT, slam is out of the question

* Your *total* points may exceed 15.

and you should sign off in 4 ♠; and you should pass a direct jump to 4 ♠.

As a second example, let's consider the various possibilities after you open with 1 ♡ holding the following 15–point hand:

> ♠ A K 8
> ♡ K Q J 6 5
> ◊ Q 10 8 3
> ♣ 7

If partner raises to 2 ♡, game should be a good bet if he has a maximum or some key values in diamonds and you should invite it by bidding 3 ◊. If instead partner responds 3 ♡, raise to 4 ♡. Pass a direct jump to 4 ♡. If partner's first response is 3 NT, slam is likely if most of his high-card points are in the red suits and you should make a mild slam try by cue-bidding 4 ◊.

Simple new suit bids by responder

If you cannot support opener's major suit, show a good four-card or longer suit of your own if you have one. You may bid a new suit at the one-level with 8 or more points, but you need at least 11 points to enter the rarefied atmosphere of the two-level. Also, a 2 ♡ response to a 1 ♠ opening bid promises at least a *five*-card suit. Some examples:

Partner's opening

1 ♠	♠ 8 3	♡ A 7 5 2	◊ A Q 8 3	♣ Q 4 2:

Bid 2 ◊, showing 11–15 points and at least four good diamonds.

1 ♠	♠ 7	♡ A Q 10 7 6	◊ A K 4 3	♣ Q 4 2:

Bid 2 ♡, promising at least five hearts and 11–15 points.

1 ♡	♠ A J 5 4 3	♡ 7	◊ K 10 3	♣ 9 7 6 2:

Bid 1 ♠, showing 8–15 points and at least four good spades.

Partner's
opening
1 ♡   ♠ A K J 10 7 6   ♡ 8 4 2   ◊ K 7   ♣ 4 3:
Bid 1 ♠. You are fully justified in giving
top billing to your own assets with such
a powerful suit. You can support hearts
next time.

After a new-suit bid by responder, opener should both define his strength and help in the quest for the proper denomination. If you are opener and have a *minimum* major-suit opening, which is defined as 11–13 *high-card* points,* convey your minimal strength to partner by refusing to bid past the level of 2 NT (unless you must do so to raise his *major* suit) :

> Make a single raise of partner's *major* suit with three-card or longer support. (If you open with 1 ♠ and partner responds 2 ♡, you may raise to 3 ♡—the only case in which you should bid past the level of 2 NT with a minimum major-suit opening.)
> Rebid a six-card or longer suit.
> Bid a new four-card or longer suit at the *two*-level.
> Bid notrump as cheaply as possible.

All of these rebids are not forcing, and responder should pass if game is out of reach and the contract is a playable one.

If instead you have a *maximum* major-suit opening, which is defined as 14–15 *high-card* points, let partner in on the good news by bidding *above* the level of 2 NT:

> *Jump* raise partner's *major* suit with three-card or longer support.
> *Jump* rebid a *good* six-card or longer suit (at least A Q J 4 3 2).

* For convenience, "minimum" and "maximum" major-suit openings are defined strictly in terms of *high-card* points. This avoids confusion that might arise from adding distribution points in some situations but not in others.

Bid a *good* new suit of four or more cards (at least
    K Q 3 2) at the *three*-level.
Raise partner's *minor* suit to the three-level with three-card
    or longer support.
Jump to 3 NT.

These rebids are forcing to game *if* responder's first bid
was at the two-level because your side must have at least 25
points (you have at least 14 and partner has at least 11). However, they are *not* forcing after a 1 ♠ response to a 1 ♡ opening,
which can be made on only 8 points, and responder should
pass if game is out of reach and the contract is a playable one.
Let's look at some examples:

	Opening Bid	Response			
1]	1 ♡	2 ♣	♠ 7	♡ A Q 8 6 5	◇ A J 6 2

♣ 6 4 3:   Bid 2 ◇. You have
a minimum major-suit opening
(11 high-card points), so
choose the most descriptive
bid that does not bypass the
level of 2 NT.

2]   1 ♡   2 ♣   ♠ A J 6 2   ♡ A Q 8 6 5   ◇ 7
♣ 6 4 3:   Bid 2 ♠.

3]   1 ♡   1 ♠   ♠ K 8 3   ♡ A Q 8 6 5   ◇ A 8 3
♣ 7 2:   Bid 2 ♠. Raise
partner's major with three-card
or longer support.

4]   1 ♡   1 ♠   ♠ 7 2   ♡ A Q 8 6 5   ◇ A 6 2
♣ Q 8 2:   Bid 1 NT. The
cheapest notrump rebid shows
a relatively balanced
minimum. If instead partner

	Opening Bid	*Response*	

had responded 2 ◊, you would bid 2 NT.

5]   1 ♡   1 ♠   ♠ 7   ♡ A Q 8 6 4 2   ◊ A 6 3 2 ♣ Q 4:   Bid 2 ♡. Prefer rebidding a six-card major to showing a new four-card minor.

6]   1 ♠   2 ♡   ♠ A Q 8 6 4   ♡ K 8 3   ◊ K J 2 ♣ 7 3:   Bid 3 ♡. The only time you may bid at the three-level with a minimum major-suit opening is when you raise responder's heart suit.

7]   1 ♡   2 ◊   ♠ 7 2   ♡ A K J 7 4   ◊ 6 3 ♣ A Q 6 3:   Bid 3 ♣. A new-suit bid at the three-level shows a maximum major-suit opening (14–15 *high-card* points) and a good suit (K Q 3 2 or better).

8]   1 ♡   2 ♣   ♠ K 10 8 7   ♡ A Q 8 6 5 ◊ A Q 3   ♣ 7:   Bid 3 ♠. A 2 ♠ bid would show a minimum, and not bidding spades at all might forever lose a 4–4 major suit fit. Therefore, you should bid 3 ♠ even though your suit is somewhat below standard.

	Opening Bid	Response	
9]	1 ♠	2 ◇	♠ A J 10 7 5　♡ A Q　◇ K 8 ♣ J 8 6 4:　Jump to 3 NT to show your maximum. Don't mind ignoring a weak *minor* suit.
10]	1 ♡	1 ♠	♠ Q 8 3　♡ A Q 7 4 3 ◇ A K 3 2　♣ 6:　Jump to 3 ♠, showing a maximum with at least three-card spade support.
11]	1 ♡	2 ♣	♠ Q 7 2　♡ Q J 10 8 5　◇ A 3 ♣ A J 7:　Raise to 3 ♣. Raising partner's suit with good support is more descriptive than jumping to 3 NT.
12]	1 ♡	2 ◇	♠ K 8　♡ A K J 7 6 3　◇ 9 7 ♣ A 10 2:　Jump to 3 ♡ to show a maximum and a good six-card or longer suit (at least A Q J 4 3 2).
13]	1 ♠	2 ♡	♠ A Q 7 6 4　♡ Q 8 6　◇ A Q 5 ♣ 6 3:　Jump to 4 ♡ to show a maximum with at least three-card heart support.

Some cases require exceptional treatment:

♠ A Q J 8 3
♡ A 8 6 4
◇ K 6 3 2
♣ ——

As we saw in Chapter 1, this hand is worth 14 points for purposes of opening the bidding, and the proper call is 1 ♠ If partner responds 2 ♡, however, you count 5 points for the club void because you intend to raise partner's suit and the value of your hand soars to 19 points! Unfortunately, you are not allowed to go back to start and change your opening bid to 1 ♣, but an effective solution is available. Since a 3 ♣ rebid would show a maximum major-suit opening, a jump to 4 ♣ can be used as a splinter bid, proudly announcing fine support for responder's suit and substantial extra values including a club void or singleton. Responder will return to 4 ♡ with only 11 or 12 points (or with wasted values in clubs) and will cuebid a new suit to invite slam with well-placed extra strength.

The forcing 1 NT response

If partner has opened with 1 ♡ or 1 ♠ and you cannot raise or show a good suit of your own, respond 1 NT. This bid is *forcing* and shows 8–15 points. For example, if partner opens with 1 ♠, bid 1 NT with each of the following hands:

♠ 7   ♡ K 8 6   ◇ A J 5 4 3   ♣ J 9 8 6:
    You have only 9 points, and you need 11 to respond at the two-level. You should also respond 1 NT with six diamonds and one less small card in a side suit.

♠ Q 3   ♡ A K 3   ◇ J 9 6 3   ♣ J 7 4 2:
    You have 11 points, but your four-card suits are pathetically weak.

After a 1 NT response, opener must rebid at or below the level of *two of his suit* if he has a minimum major-suit opening (11–13 high-card points). If he cannot bid a new four-card or longer suit at the proper level, he should choose a better three-card minor; otherwise, he should rebid his suit. After a minimum rebid, any simple suit bid by responder is a signoff, and 2 NT or a jump bid is invitational to game.

With a maximum major-suit opening (14–15 high-card

points), opener should bid *above* the level of two of his suit after a 1 NT response. He can bid a good new four-card or longer suit at the three-level (or reverse to 2 ♠ after a 1 ♡ opening), jump rebid a six-card or longer suit, or raise to 2 NT. Some examples:

Opener (you)	Responder
1 ♡	1 NT
?	

♠ 7 3   ♡ A Q 8 6 5   ◇ A Q 3   ♣ J 4 2:
> *Bid* 2 ◇. Keep the bidding at or below the level of two of your suit with a minimum, and choose your stronger three-card minor.

♠ K J 8 7   ♡ A K 8 6 5   ◇ 7 2   ♣ 5 4:
> *Bid* 2 ♡. Although it is usually best to avoid rebidding a five-card suit after a 1 NT response, you have no choice in this instance. It would be even worse to bid a two-card minor, and a 2 ♠ bid would show a maximum major-suit opening.

♠ 8 6 3   ♡ A K 8 6 5   ◇ A K J 7   ♣ 4:
> *Jump to* 3 ◇ to show a maximum major-suit opening with a good four-card or longer diamond suit.

♠ K 6 3   ♡ A K 7 6 3   ◇ A 10 3   ♣ 7 2:
> *Bid* 2 NT, showing a maximum with no good new suit to bid.

♠ K 6 3   ♡ A K 7 5 4 2   ◇ A 10   ♣ 7 2:
> *Jump to* 3 ♡ to show a maximum with a six-card or longer suit.

♠ K J 8 7   ♡ A Q 8 6 5   ◇ 7 2   ♣ A 8:
> *Bid* 2 ♠. Any new suit bid above the level of two of your own suit shows a maximum major-suit opening.

♠ A K 7   ♡ A K J 8 5   ◊ 9 5 4 2   ♣ 6:
Bid 2 NT. Refuse to mention the abysmal diamond suit.

All rebids by opener after a 1 NT response are *not* forcing, and responder should pass with no chance for game if the contract is a playable one. Otherwise, responder should have enough information to select an appropriate signoff (having denied three-card or longer support, he may return to opener's suit with two-card support), invite game, or bid game directly if he can determine that your side must have at least 25 points

Responses to 1♥ and 1♠ opening bids with 16 or more high-card points

If partner opens with 1 ♡ or 1 ♠ and you have 16 or more high-card points, slam is a definite possibility. Quickly alert partner to this important news by either jumping in a new suit or jumping to 2 NT.

Jump shifts by responder

A jump in a new suit after a 1 ♡ or 1 ♠ opening bid is forcing to game and shows 16 or more high-card points and a good five-card or longer suit. It may conceal good support for opener's suit. With 19 or more high-card points, you may jump shift even if your five-card or longer suit is mediocre. For example, suppose that partner opens with 1 ♡ and you are fortunate enough to hold any of the following hands:

♠ A K J 10 7   ♡ K 4 3   ◊ A J 9 2   ♣ 4:
Jump to 2 ♠.

♠ A J 6 2   ♡ A 7   ◊ K 6   ♣ K Q J 9 5:
Jump to 3 ♣.

♠ Q 8 6 5 2   ♡ A 7   ◊ A K 3   ♣ A K 2:
Jump to 2 ♠. Having 19 or more high-card points will compensate for the mediocre spade suit.

♠ A K Q 9 8 6   ♡ 7   ◇ A K 3   ♣ 7 4 2:
Jump to 2 ♠. The superb spade suit will compensate for the poor fit with opener's heart suit.

♠ A Q 10 8 6 5   ♡ A Q 6 2   ◇ K 3   ♣ 7:
Jump to 2 ♠. Although you have only 15 high-card points, you have a fine spade suit and powerful heart support. A splinter bid in clubs would conceal the spades and thoroughly confuse the bidding, and a 1 ♠ response would be a monstrous underbid that would cause enormous difficulties on your next turn.

♠ A Q 8 6 2   ♡ 7   ◇ K J 7 2   ♣ A Q 2:
Devalue your hand and bid 1 ♠. You have only 16 high-card points, the singleton in partner's suit may well hinder both the bidding and the play, and your hand doesn't have any important redeeming feature (such as an excellent suit with considerable trick-taking power).

After a jump shift response, opener should show three-card or longer support for responder's suit by making a single raise. With poor support, opener should rebid notrump as cheaply as possible with a minimum balanced hand, bid a good new four-card or longer suit, or rebid his own suit. The first duty facing the partnership is to locate a good trump suit; then, slam may be explored by cue-bidding if either partner has extra values.*

The 2 NT response

A 2 NT response to a 1 ♡ or 1 ♠ opening bid shows 16 or more high-card points and no good five-card or longer suit. Like the jump shift, it is forcing to game and strongly invitational to slam. For example, if partner opens with 1 ♠, bid 2 NT with either of the following hands:

---

* Alternatively, an asking-bid structure may be used after a jump shift response. See Chapter 12.

♠ A 8 6 3   ♠ A K 3
♡ Q 8 2   ♡ J 4
◇ A K 3   ◇ K Q 10 7
♣ K J 7   ♣ A K J 2

However, *don't* bid 2 NT with a hand such as

♠ A Q 8 6
♡ A J 5 3
◇ K 6 3 2
♣ 4

while you have 17 points in support of spades (counting 3 points for the singleton club), you have only 14 high-card points. As we saw earlier in this chapter, the ideal solution is to make a splinter bid of 4 ♣, showing 11–15 high card points, excellent support for opener's suit, and a singleton or void in clubs.

If the 2 NT bidder has three-card or longer support for opener's major suit, he should show it on his next turn to bid. After the 2 NT response, opener should rebid 3 NT with a minimum balanced hand, make a conventional 3 ♣ bid to show a minimum unbalanced hand, rebid his suit with a balanced maximum, and bid a good new four-card or longer suit with an unbalanced maximum. After a good trump suit is found, cue-bidding may be used to exchange information about slam prospects.

When the opponents interfere

After a takeout double

If a 1 ♡ or 1 ♠ opening bid is followed by a takeout double, many experts prefer to use direct raises as preemptive bids designed to blockade the opponents and make it difficult for them to find their best contract. These preemptive raises show a maximum of 7 points and good support for opener's suit; the better the support, the higher the level at which the preemptive raise can be made. A 1 NT response after a takeout double is used to show a normal raise to the two-level, while a 2 NT response shows a normal raise to the three-level. A redouble shows 11 or more points and expresses a desire to penalize the opponents when they subsequently remove the redouble to a contract of their own. Other bids retain the normal meaning after a takeout double.

After an overcall

If a 1 ♡ or 1 ♠ opening bid is followed by an overcall, raises retain the usual meaning. Precision recommends using a 1 NT response to show 8–10 high-card points and at least one stopper in the enemy suit, and a 2 NT response to show 11–12 high-card points and at least one stopper in the opponents' suit. These notrump responses are natural and *not* forcing. A cuebid of the enemy suit shows 11 or more high-card points and good support for opener's suit, and is forcing. Finally, a double is negative and guarantees four cards in the unbid major; opener should not pass unless his own hand calls for a penalty double. Other bids retain the normal meaning after an overcall.

Auctions after a 1♥ or 1♠ opening bid

Opening bid of 1♥ or 1♠ = 11–15 points, five-card or longer suit

Responder's bid	Opener's rebid
Pass = 0–7 points, (usually) a poor fit for opener's suit.	
Single raise = 8–10 points, at least three-card support. Not forcing.	Any bid = maximum, game try. New suit shows where help will be most valuable.
Jump raise = 11–13 points, at least three-card support. Not forcing.	Pass with 11–12 points; raise to game with 13–15 points.
3 NT = 14–15 points, good three-card or better support. Forcing.	Raise to game = signoff; new suit = maximum, slam try.
Triple raise = 14–15 points, maximum of 10 high-card points, four-card or better support. Not forcing.	New suit = slam try.
Double jump in new suit = *splinter bid* showing 11–15 *high-card* points, good three-card support or better, *singleton or void* in bid suit.	Game bid in opener's suit = signoff; new suit = slam try.
Simple New Suit Bid: Usually denies good support for	MINIMUM major-suit opening (11–13 *high-card* points):

Responder's bid	Opener's rebid

opener's suit. 2-over-1
= 11–15 points, good
four-card or longer suit
(2 ♡ response to 1 ♠
promises at least a five-card
suit), forcing. 1 ♠ response
to 1 ♡ = 8–15 points, good
four-card or longer
suit. Forcing.

Raise responder's *major*
  suit.
Rebid a 6-card or longer
  suit.
Bid a new four-card or
  longer suit below the
  level of 2 NT.
Bid notrump as cheaply as
  possible.
MAXIMUM major-suit opening
  (14–15 *high-card* points):
Jump raise responder's
  major suit.
Jump rebid a *good* 6-card
  or longer suit (at least
  A Q J 4 3 2).
Bid a *good* new four-card
  or longer suit (at least
  K Q 3 2) at the *three*-level.
Raise responder's *minor*
  suit.
Jump to 3 NT.

1 NT = 8–15 points, poor
  support for opener's suit,
  no good new suit. Forcing.

MINIMUM major-suit opening
  (11–13 *high-card* points):
Bid new four-card or longer
  suit *below* the level of
  two of opener's first suit.
Bid a better three-card
  minor.
Rebid original suit.
MAXIMUM major-suit opening
  (14–15 *high-card* points):
Bid a *good* new four-card
  or longer suit (at least
  K Q 3 2) *above* the level

Responder's bid	*Opener's rebid*
	of two of opener's first suit. *Jump* rebid a *good* 6-card or longer suit (at least A Q J 4 3 2). Raise to 2 NT.
Jump in New Suit = 16 or more high-card points, good five-card or longer suit. May have good support for opener's suit.	Raise with three-card or longer suit; with poor support, bid 3 NT with balanced minimum, and otherwise bid a good new four-card or longer suit or rebid original suit.
Jump to 2 NT = 16 or more high-card points, no good new suit. May have good support for opener's suit.	3 NT = balanced minimum. 3 ♣ = unbalanced minimum. Rebid of original suit = balanced maximum. New suit = natural, unbalanced maximum.

REVIEW QUIZ

PART I.

What is your opening bid in each of the following problems?

1] ♠ J 10 9 7 4   2] ♠ Q J   3] ♠ K Q 8 7 6   4] ♠ K 8 6 3
   ♡ 6   ♡ Q J 6 4 3   ♡ Q 10 8 6 5 3   ♡ A Q 10 7
   ◊ A Q 8 6 5   ◊ Q 5 2   ◊ A   ♡ 3 2
   ♣ A K   ♣ Q J 3   ♣ 7   ♣ K J 6

PART II.

Opener's bid is shown in each of the following problems. What is your response?

5] Opener's Bid 1 ♡   6] Opener's Bid 1 ♠   7] Opener's Bid 1 ♠
   ♠ K 8   ♠ Q 7 3   ♠ 9 7 5
   ♡ A 7 2   ♡ A K J 9 6 3   ♡ 6 2
   ◊ K 8 4 3   ◊ A Q 6   ◊ 9 8 7 4
   ♣ J 10 7 2   ♣ 3   ♣ A Q 4 3

8] Opener's Bid 1 ♠   9] Opener's Bid 1 ♡   10] Opener's Bid 1 ♡
   ♠ K 8 7 3 2   ♠ A Q 3   ♠ A K 5
   ♡ Q 10 5 3   ♡ 8 7   ♡ Q 7 6
   ◊ A 5 3 2   ◊ A Q 9 8   ◊ J 9 8 4 3
   ♣ --   ♣ J 8 4 3   ♣ A K

11] Opener's Bid 1 ♠   12] Opener's Bid 1 ♡   13] Opener's Bid 1 ♡
    ♠ Q 10 8 6   ♠ K 8 2   ♠ A K J 7
    ♡ A 7   ♡ 7 3   ♡ 6
    ◊ K Q 8 5   ◊ A J 5 2   ◊ Q 8 5 2
    ♣ K 7 4   ♣ Q 6 4 2   ♣ 10 9 7 5

14] Opener's Bid 1 ♠
    ♠ K Q 8 6
    ♡ A J 7 3
    ◊ 8
    ♣ K J 6 3

PRECISION SYSTEM

PART III.

The opening bid and first response are shown in each of the following problems, and you are asked to select opener's rebid. Where two responses are shown, determine your answer for each one.

15] Opening Bid   Response
   1 ♡   1 ♠
  ♠ Q 6
  ♡ A J 7 4 2
  ◇ K 8 3
  ♣ K 9 2

16] Opening Bid   Response
   1 ♠   (a) 2 ◇
              (b) 1 NT
  ♠ K Q J 6 2
  ♡ A 7 3
  ◇ 8 2
  ♣ K Q 5

17] Opening Bid   Response
   1 ♠   (a) 2 ♣
              (b) 1 NT
  ♠ A 10 9 7 3
  ♡ K J 8 2
  ◇ K 6
  ♣ 7 5

18] Opening Bid   Response
   1 ♡   (a) 2 ◇
              (b) 1 NT
  ♠ K Q 7 3
  ♡ K J 7 5 4
  ◇ 4 2
  ♣ K 10

19] Opening Bid   Response
   1 ♡   3 ♣
  ♠ K J 7
  ♡ A Q 10 9 3
  ◇ Q 10 3
  ♣ 3 2

20] Opening Bid   Response
   1 ♠   (a) 2 ♡
              (b) 1 NT
  ♠ Q 10 7 6 4
  ♡ A J 7 6
  ◇ K 4
  ♣ A 4

21] Opening Bid   Response
   1 ♡   (a) 2 ◇
              (b) 1 NT
  ♠ A Q 7
  ♡ K 10 4 3 2
  ◇ 6
  ♣ A Q 8 4

22] Opening Bid   Response
   1 ♡   (a) 2 ♣
              (b) 1 NT
  ♠ K Q 2
  ♡ A J 8 7 4 3
  ◇ J 6 3
  ♣ J

23] Opening Bid   Response
   1 ♡   (a) 2 ♣
              (b) 1 NT
  ♠ A 10 7 5
  ♡ Q J 7 4 2
  ◇ A 4
  ♣ A 6

24] Opening Bid   Response
   1 ♡   (a) 1 ♠
              (b) 1 NT
  ♠ J 6 2
  ♡ K Q J 4 3
  ◇ A 9
  ♣ 10 3 2

25] Opening Bid   Response
   1 ♠   (a) 2 ◇
              (b) 1 NT
  ♠ K 8 6 3 2
  ♡ A Q 3
  ◇ 9 3 2
  ♣ K J

26] Opening Bid   Respons‐
   1 ♡   2 ♠
  ♠ J 7 4
  ♡ A J 10 6 5
  ◇ A Q 8 3
  ♣ 7

27] Opening Bid Response
  1 ♠   (a) 2 ♣
              (b) 1 NT
  ♠ A K J 9 8 3
  ♡ 8 2
  ◇ A Q 3
  ♣ 6 5

28] Opening Bid Response
  1 ♠   2 ♡
  ♠ A J 8 5 2
  ♡ K 7 5
  ◇ 7 3
  ♣ A 10 8

29] Opening Bid Response
  1 ♠   2 NT
  ♠ A J 7 4 3
  ♡ K 8 3
  ◇ Q 3
  ♣ Q 10 9

30] Opening Bid Response
  1 ♡   (a) 1 ♠
              (b) 1 NT
  ♠ K Q 7
  ♡ A K Q 6 2
  ◇ 7
  ♣ 10 8 7 5

Solutions

1] *One spade.* With two five-card suits, bid the higher-ranking suit.

2] *Pass.* This miserable collection of queens and jacks is *not* worth 11 points!

3] *One heart.* Open in your longest suit.

4] *One notrump.* Don't open a four-card major suit.

5] *Three hearts.* You have 12 points in support of hearts. Don't bother with sketchy side suits when you can raise opener's major.

6] *Three hearts.* A minimum jump shift—16 high-card points and a good five-card or longer suit.

7] *Pass.* You have only 7 points in support of spades.

8] *Four spades.* The triple raise shows 14–15 total points, a maximum of 10 high-card points, and four-card or longer support. Don't make a splinter bid unless you have at least 11 high-card points.

9] *Two diamonds.* With 13 points, you are strong enough to respond at the two-level and you have a good suit to mention.

10] *Two notrump.* Shows at least 16 high-card points and no suit worthy of a jump shift.

11] *Three notrump.* Shows a strong spade raise and is forcing.

12] *One notrump.* You need 11 points to respond at the two-level.

13] *One spade.* Show your fine four-card suit.

14] *Four diamonds.* A splinter bid showing 11–15 high-card points, good spade support, and a void or singleton in diamonds.

15] *One notrump.* Shows a minimum major-suit opening (11–13 high-card points) with no good new suit to bid.

16] a) *Three notrump.* After a new suit response, you must bid above the level of 2 NT to show a maximum major-suit opening (14–15 high-card points).

b) *Two notrump.* After a 1 NT response, any bid above the level of two of opener's original suit shows a maximum.

17] a) *and* b) *Two hearts.* Simply bid your four-card heart suit with a minimum.

18] a) *Two spades.* After a new suit response, any bid at or below the level of 2 NT shows a minimum, so you may mention your spade suit.

b) *Two hearts.* After a 1 NT response, a reverse to 2 ♠ would show a maximum, and you have no three-card minor to bid.

19] *Three notrump.* After a jump shift, a 3 NT rebid shows a balanced minimum with poor support for responder's suit.

20] a) *Four hearts.* Jump raise to show a maximum.

b) *Three hearts.* Jump to show a maximum.

21] a) *and* b) *Three clubs.* Bidding a new suit at the three-level shows a maximum and a good four-card or longer suit.

22] a) and b) *Two hearts.* Shows a six-card or longer suit and a minimum.

23] a) *Three spades.* Show your spades to help locate a 4–4 major-suit fit, and jump to show a maximum.

b) *Two spades.* After a 1 NT response, a reverse to 2 ♠ shows a maximum.

24] a) *Two spades.* Raise partner's major with three-card or longer support.

b) *Two clubs.* After a 1 NT response, don't bid above the level of two of your original suit. It is better to show a three-card minor than to rebid a five-card suit.

25] a) *Two notrump.* A diamond raise would show a maximum, and a spade rebid would promise a six-card or longer suit.

b) *Two diamonds.* The clubs may seem stronger, but don't bid a two-card minor after a 1 NT response.

26] *Three spades.* After a jump shift, raise with three-card or longer support to fix the trump suit.

27] *a)* and *b)* *Three spades.* The most impressive feature of your hand is the fine spade suit. Jump to show a maximum with a six-card or longer suit.

28] *Three hearts.* Partner's response promises at least a five-card suit, so three-card support is sufficient.

29] *Three notrump.* This bid tells your partner that you have a balanced minimum.

30] *a) Three spades.* Jump raise partner's major suit with a maximum.

b) Two notrump. A much better way of showing a maximum than bidding the miserable club suit at the three-level.

8

Auctions after a 1♦ opening bid

The 1♦ opening bid

A PRECISION OPENING BID of 1 ◊ shows 11–15 points and a four-card or longer diamond suit. For example:

♠ K 8 6 3   ♡ K 10 8 7   ◊ A Q 6 2   ♣ 3:
Open 1 ◊. A major-suit opening would promise at least a five-card suit.

♠ 3   ♡ A J 10 9 7   ◊ A Q 9 8 6 4   ♣ 5:
Open 1 ◊, bidding your longest suit at the one-level.

♠ 4   ♡ A K 3   ◊ A J 10 5   ♣ Q 7 6 4 3:
Open 1 ◊. A natural club opening bid must be made at the *two*-level, so prefer any reasonable alternative if clubs are weak.

Responses to a 1♦ opening bid with 0–15 high-card points

When responder should pass

As we saw in the last chapter, there is no need to grimly scrape up a response with a weak hand after a *limited* Precision opening bid. If partner opens with 1 ◊, you should usually pass with 0–7 points:

♠ 8 6 3 2   ♡ 7 5 4 2   ◊ 3 2   ♣ Q 8 3:
Pass.

♠ Q 8 6 3 2   ♡ Q 3 2   ◇ 8 6 5   ♣ Q 10:
> *Pass.* Looking for a better contract could cause serious trouble, and has little to gain since game is hopelessly out of reach.

Major-suit responses

As the name implies, *minor* suits are second-class citizens in the world of bridge. Lest this arouse any undue sympathy, note that this lowly status is well-deserved! A minor-suit game requires you to exert yourself to the utmost and bring home 11 tricks, while 10 tricks will suffice for game in a major suit and only 9 tricks will be enough for a notrump game. Thus, while you should rush to raise partner's *major*-suit opening bid if you have adequate support, take a much dimmer view of raising a 1 ◇ opening bid.

One superior plan is to introduce a good new major suit if you have one. In Precision, a 1 ♡ or 1 ♠ response to a 1 ◇ opening bid is forcing and shows 8–15 points and a four-card or longer suit. For example, if partner opens with 1 ◇, respond as follows:

♠ Q 10 7 3   ♡ 7   ◇ K Q 6 2   ♣ J 8 4 2:
> *Bid* 1 ♠.

♠ K 10 7 6   ♡ Q 10 7 5   ◇ A 3   ♣ A 7 4:
> *Bid* 1 ♡. With two *four*-card major suits, leave room for partner to mention spades at the one-level.

♠ A Q 10 7 5   ♡ A J 7 6 3   ◇ 6   ♣ 3 2:
> *Bid* 1 ♠. With two *five*-card (or two six-card) suits, bid the higher-ranking suit. When you next bid hearts, partner can return to spades cheaply if he prefers that suit.

♠ K Q 8 6   ♡ 7 2   ◇ 6 3   ♣ A Q J 6 3:
> *Bid* 1 ♠. In Precision, a 2 ♣ response usually denies a four-card or longer major suit.

PRECISION SYSTEM

After a 1 ◊ opening bid and a major-suit response, the subsequent bidding is natural and straightforward. If you are opener and have a *minimum* 1 ◊ opening bid (defined as 11–13 *high-card* points), take one of the following conservative actions:

Raise responder's major suit with four-card or longer support.

Bid 1 ♠ after a 1 ♡ response with a four-card or longer spade suit.

Rebid a six-card or longer diamond suit.

Bid 1 NT with a relatively balanced hand.

Bid 2 ♣ with a four-card or longer club suit and an unbalanced hand (at least 5-4-3-1 distribution).

All of these limited rebids are not forcing. If responder wishes to insist on reaching game in spite of your pessimistic message, he must either bid game directly (a signoff) or *jump* in a new suit. Any other rebid by responder is *not* forcing.*

If you are blessed with a *maximum* 1 ◊ opening (14–15 *high-card* points), inform partner of this cheery news by selecting one of the following actions:

Jump raise partner's major suit with four-card or longer support.

Bid a *good* new four-card or longer suit *above* the level of 2 ◊.

Jump rebid a good six-card or longer diamond suit.

Jump to 3 ♣ with a minor two-suiter (5–5 or better).

Jump to 2 NT.

After a maximum rebid, any new-suit bid by responder is forcing for one round, any jump in a new suit is forcing to game, and any game bid is a signoff. Other bids are not forcing.

Let's look at a few examples:

---

* An exception: After a 1 NT rebid by opener, a jump return to 3 ◊ by responder is forcing.

         Opener (you)   Responder
            1 ◊   1 ♡
            ?

♠ K 8 6 3   ♡ K 10 8 7   ◊ A Q 6 2   ♣ 3:
Raise to 2 ♡ to show a minimum 1 ◊ opening (11–13 high-card points) and at least four-card support.

♠ K J 6 3   ♡ 8 7   ◊ A K 8 6 3 2   ♣ 5:
Bid 1 ♠. Prefer showing a respectable new major suit to rebidding a six-card diamond suit.

♠ Q 10 3   ♡ 10 8 2   ◊ A Q 10 9 2   ♣ K 3
Bid 1 NT.

♠ 8 6 3   ♡ A   ◊ K Q 10 8 4 3   ♣ Q J 2:
Bid 2 ◊.

♠ 7 4 3   ♡ 2   ◊ A Q 9 8 6   ♣ A K 10 4:
Bid 2 ♣.

♠ K 8   ♡ K Q 8 7   ◊ A Q 5 4 3   ♣ 7 4:
Jump raise to 3 ♡ to show a maximum 1 ◊ opening (14–15 high-card points) and at least four-card support.

♠ K J 10 2   ♡ Q 3 2   ◊ A K J 7 5   ♣ 2:
Jump to 2 ♠.

♠ A J 3   ♡ 7   ◊ K Q J 6 3   ♣ K J 3 2:
Jump to 2 NT.

♠ 8   ♡ K 6 2   ◊ A Q J 9 7 6   ♣ K J 4:
Jump to 3 ◊.

♠ K 3   ♡ 6   ◊ A Q J 5 4   ♣ A J 6 4 2:
Jump to 3 ♣ to show a maximum minor two-suiter.

Minor-suit responses

If you can't bid a major suit after partner's 1 ◊ opening bid, the next best choice is to raise diamonds. In Precision, a jump raise to 3 ◊ is a signoff, showing a weak hand with at least five-card diamond support. A single raise to 2 ◊ shows 11–15 *high-card* points and at least four-card diamond support and is forcing for one round. For example, if partner opens with 1 ◊, respond as follows:

♠ —   ♡ 7 3 2   ◊ K J 6 5 4   ♣ J 8 6 3 2:
Sign off by raising to 3 ◊. This preemptive action figures to be safe and will make it extremely difficult for the opponents to enter the auction.

♠ 6 4   ♡ A 7 3   ◊ A Q 8 6   ♣ J 10 4 2:
Raise to 2 ◊. You have 11 high-card points, four-card diamond support, and no four-card or longer major suit.

♠ 6   ♡ A 6 3   ◊ K J 8 7 5   ♣ A Q 4 2:
Raise to 2 ◊. The single raise is forcing for one round, so you have time to make certain that game is reached.

After a raise to 2 ◊, opener should help investigate the possibility of playing in 3 NT by rebidding as follows:

Minimum 1 ◊ opening (11–13 High-Card Points)	*Maximum 1 ◊ opening* (14–15 High-Card Points)
2 ♡ = heart stopper, no spade stopper.	3 ♡ = heart stopper, no spade stopper.
2 ♠ = spade stopper, no heart stopper.	3 ♠ = spade stopper, no heart stopper.
2 NT = stoppers in both majors.	3 NT = stoppers in both majors.
3 ◊ = no stopper in either major.	3 ♣ = no stopper in either major.

Here are some examples of these useful rebids in action:

Opener	Responder	Opener	Responder
♠ K 8 3	♠ A Q 5	1 ◊	2 ◊
♡ 7 2	♡ 6 4	2 ♠	3 ◊
◊ A Q 8 6 5	◊ K J 7 4	Pass	
♣ K 6 2	♣ Q 10 5 3		

Opener's rebid of 2 ♠ shows a minimum, a stopper in spades, and no heart stopper. After such an explicit message, responder has no difficulty deciding to sign off in 3 ◊.

Opener	Responder	Opener	Responder
♠ K 8 3	♠ 6 4	1 ◊	2 ◊
♡ 7 2	♡ A J 6	2 ♠	3 ♠
◊ A Q 8 6 5	◊ K J 7 4	3 NT	Pass
♣ K 6 2	♣ A Q 5 4		

This time, opener's spade stopper is just what responder needs. To be sure that the notrump game is played from the right side, responder bids 3 ♠. This cannot be an attempt to play in spades because responder's 2 ◊ bid denies a four-card major, so opener obliges by bidding the laydown notrump game.

Opener	Responder	Opener	Responder
♠ 6 5 2	♠ A K 8	1 ◊	2 ◊
♡ 7	♡ A J 10	3 ♣	3 NT
◊ A K J 7 3	◊ 10 6 4 2		
♣ A Q 10 3	♣ 7 6 4		

Opener's 3 ♣ rebid shows a maximum hand with no major-suit stoppers. Responder can count at least 26 high-card points in the two hands and is not worried about the major suits, so he readily contracts for the excellent notrump game.

Opener	Responder	Opener	Responder
♠ 6 5 2	♠ A K 8	1 ◊	2 ◊
♡ 7	♡ 9 5 2	3 ♣	4 ◊
◊ A K J 7 3	◊ Q 10 6 4	5 ◊	Pass
♣ A Q 7 3	♣ K 8 5		

This time, responder properly fears the heart suit and elects to try for game in diamonds. Opener's valuable fifth card in diamonds is sufficient reason to accept responder's invitation.

If partner opens with 1 ◊ and you cannot show a major suit or raise diamonds, a 2 ♣ response may be just what the doctor ordered. As always, a two-over-one response is forcing and requires at least 11 points:

    ♠ 8 3   ♡ A 6 2   ◊ 6 4 3   ♣ A Q J 7 2:
        Respond 2 ♣.

    ♠ 10 7 6 5   ♡ 6   ◊ A 3   ♣ A K 9 8 6 4:
        Respond 2 ♣. Bidding the weak four-card spade suit ahead of the fine six-card club suit would be carrying a principle much too far! If opener has a good spade suit, he will bid it.

After a 2 ♣ response, opener should show his stoppers in much the same way as after a forcing raise to 2 ◊. There is one change in the procedures: Opener should bid 2 ◊ to show a minimum with no stoppers in the major suits.

NT responses

After a 1 ◊ opening bid, a 1 NT response shows 8–10 high-card points, balanced suit distribution, and no four-card or longer major suit. It is *not* forcing. A jump to 3 NT shows similar distribution and 14–15 high-card points. For example, suppose that partner opens with 1 ◊ and you hold:

    ♠ K 10 3   ♡ Q 8 3   ◊ Q 6 3   ♣ J 10 4 2:
        Respond 1 NT.

    ♠ A Q 7   ♡ K J 2   ◊ 10 9 7   ♣ K Q 5 2:
        Respond 3 NT.

    ♠ K J 3   ♡ A Q 10   ◊ K 4   ♣ J 8 6 4 3:
        Respond 3 NT. *Don't bid the weak ♣ suit.*

Opener will usually pass these natural notrump responses. However, he will bid a new suit over a 1 NT response with a very distributional hand that is not suitable for notrump play, and will raise to 2 NT with a 15-point maximum to invite game in notrump.

Responses to a 1♦ opening bid with 16 or more high-card points

Responses to a 1 ◊ opening bid with 16 or more high-card points are virtually identical to those discussed in the preceding chapter. That is, you should jump in a good new five-card or longer suit if you have one; if not, jump to 2 NT. For example, suppose that partner opens with 1 ◊ and you are the lucky holder of either of the following hands:

♠ A K J 9 7 ♡ A K 6 ◊ Q 8 3 ♣ 7 3:
Jump to 2 ♠.

♠ K Q 10 7 ♡ A K 3 ◊ K Q 8 5 ♣ K 7:
Jump to 2 NT.

These responses are forcing to game and strongly invitational to slam. Opener's rebids are similar to those presented in the preceding chapter: After a jump shift, he should raise with three-card or longer support to fix the trump suit; with poor support, opener bids 3 NT with a balanced minimum, bids a good new four-card or longer suit, or rebids 3 ◊. After a 2 NT response, opener rebids 3 ♣ to show an unbalanced minimum, bids 3 NT to show a balanced minimum, chooses 3 ◊ to show a balanced maximum, and bids a new suit to show an unbalanced maximum.

When the opponents interfere

If the opponents enter the auction after a 1 ◊ opening bid, most responses retain the usual meaning. After a takeout double, a redouble promises at least 11 high-card points and indicates a desire to penalize the opponents when they escape to a suit of their own. After an overcall, a double at the two-level is negative and shows at least one four-card major suit, but a double at the three-level or higher is for penalties. A cue-bid of the enemy suit is forcing and promises at least 11 high-card points, and asks opener to show a good new four-card or longer suit if he has one.

Auctions after a 1♦ opening bid

Opening bid of 1 ◇ = 11–15 points, four-card or longer suit.

Responder's bid	*Opener's rebid*

Pass = 0–7 points.

1 ♡ or 1 ♠ = 8–15 points, four-card or longer suit. Forcing.

MINIMUM 1 ◇ opening (11–13 *high-card* points):

Raise responder's major with four-card or longer support.

Bid 1 ♠ after a 1 ♡ response with a four-card or longer spade suit.

Rebid a six-card or longer diamond suit.

Bid 1 NT with a balanced hand.

Bid 2 ♣ with four or more clubs and an unbalanced hand (at least 5-4-3-1 distribution).

MAXIMUM 1 ◇ opening (14–15 *high-card* points):

Jump raise responder's major with four-card or longer support.

Bid a *good* new four-card or longer suit *above* the level of 2 ◇.

Jump rebid a good six-card or longer diamond suit.

Jump to 3 ♣ with a minor

Responder's bid	*Opener's rebid*
	two-suiter (at least 5–5). *Jump* to 2 NT.
1 NT = 8–10 points, no four-card or longer major suit, balanced hand. Not forcing.	2 NT = 15-point maximum, invitational to 3 NT. New suit = very distributional hand not suitable for notrump play.

2 ♢ = 11–15 points, no four-card or longer major suit, at least four-card diamond support. Forcing.	MINIMUM 1 ♢ opening (11–13 high-card points):
	  2 ♡ = heart stopper, no spade stopper.
	  2 ♠ = spade stopper, no heart stopper.
	  2 NT = stoppers in both majors.
	  3 ♢ = no stopper in either major.
	MAXIMUM 1 ♢ opening (14–15 high-card points):
	  3 ♡ = heart stopper, no spade stopper.
	  3 ♠ = spade stopper, no heart stopper.
	  3 NT = stoppers in both majors.
	  3 ♣ = no stopper in either major.

2 ♣ = 11–15 points, (usually) no four-card or longer major suit, good four-card or longer club suit. (May have good six-card or	Similar to rebids after a 2 ♢ response except that 2 ♢ rebid = minimum with no stopper in either major.

Responder's bid	*Opener's rebid*

longer club suit and weak
four-card major.) Forcing.

3 ◊ = signoff; weak hand with
five-card or longer
diamond support.

3 NT = 14–15 points, no
four-card or longer major
suit, balanced hand. Not
forcing.

Jump in new suit = 16 or more high-card points, good five-card or longer suit. Forcing to game.	Raise with three-card or longer support to fix the trump suit. With poor support, bid 3 NT with a balanced minimum, and otherwise bid a good new four-card or longer suit or rebid 3 ◊.
2 NT = 16 or more high-card points, no good five-card or longer suit. Forcing to game.	3 NT = balanced minimum. 3 ♣ − unbalanced minimum. 3 ◊ = balanced maximum. New suit = unbalanced maximum.

REVIEW QUIZ

PART I.

What is your opening bid in each of the following problems?

1] ♠ K J 8 6   2] ♠ A Q 8 6 5   3] ♠ A 7   4] ♠ A 8 3
   ♡ A K Q 7   ♡ K 3   ♡ K Q 3   ♡ 7 2
   ◇ Q 10 8 3   ◇ A 10 8 7 6 ◇ A K J 8 6 2 ◇ K Q 10 8 6 5
   ♣ 6   ♣ 10   ♣ 8 4   ♣ Q 10

PART II.

Partner opens with 1 ◇ in each of the following problems. What is your response?

5] ♠ 7   6] ♠ A J 8   7] ♠ K 8 3
   ♡ K 10 6 2   ♡ 9 7 3   ♡ K 2
   ◇ A J 8 3   ◇ K 9 8 3   ◇ Q 10 3
   ♣ 10 9 8 2   ♣ K J 2   ♣ J 9 6 3 2

8] ♠ 7   9] ♠ J 8 6   10] ♠ A Q 10 7 5
   ♡ A K Q 5 4 2   ♡ Q 10 7 4 3   ♡ A K J 7 3
   ◇ 7 5   ◇ 8 6 3   ◇ 6
   ♣ A K J 8   ♣ K 2   ♣ 3 2

11] ♠ K Q 3   12] ♠ K 8 3   13] ♠ K Q 8
   ♡ A Q 3   ♡ 7   ♡ A Q 8
   ◇ 7 6 5   ◇ Q J 9 8 6 2 ◇ K J 6 3
   ♣ K 10 7 2   ♣ 10 5 3   ♣ A 7 3

14] ♠ K 6 3
   ♡ Q 7 2
   ◇ 7
   ♣ A K J 8 6 3

PART III.

You have opened the bidding with 1 ◇ and partner has made the response shown. What is your rebid in each of the following problems?

15] Response 1 ♠
- ♠ 7
- ♡ K 8 6 3
- ◊ K J 8 7 2
- ♣ A 10 3

16] Response 2 ♣
- ♠ A Q 8
- ♡ 7 4 3
- ◊ A J 10 6 5 2
- ♣ 9

17] Response 1 ♡
- ♠ K 8 6 3
- ♡ J 2
- ◊ A K 4 3 2
- ♣ Q 8

18] Response 1 ♠
- ♠ 7 3 2
- ♡ A 6
- ◊ A Q 10 8 7 2
- ♣ Q 7

19] Response 2 ◊
- ♠ A Q 8
- ♡ A J 7 2
- ◊ K J 7 5 3
- ♣ 6

20] Response 1 ♡
- ♠ A K 7 4
- ♡ 8 6 5 4
- ◊ K 10 6 5
- ♣ A

21] Response 2 ◊
- ♠ 8 7 2
- ♡ K Q 3
- ◊ A K Q 6 4 2
- ♣ 3

22] Response 1 ♡
- ♠ A J 10 7
- ♡ 6 2
- ◊ K Q J 8 5
- ♣ K 2

23] Response 2 ◊
- ♠ 6 3
- ♡ 7 2
- ◊ A K Q 6 5 2
- ♣ A Q 8

24] Response 1 ♠
- ♠ K 8
- ♡ Q 7
- ◊ K J 10 6 5
- ♣ K 10 8 2

25] Response 2 ♣
- ♠ K 8 3
- ♡ K J 6
- ◊ A 9 8 7 6 5
- ♣ 2

Solutions

1] *One diamond.* A typical 1 ◊ opening bid.

2] *One spade.* Bid your higher-ranking five-card suit.

3] *One club.* Remember to select the 1 ♣ opening with 16 or more points.

4] *One diamond.* Since the 1 ◊ opening bid is limited, you can open with hands such as this without worrying that partner will get carried away. This enables you to describe your hand to partner and thoroughly interfere with the opponents' bidding machinery.

5] *One heart.* If partner's rebid does not represent a playable contract, sign off in diamonds on your next turn.

6] *Two diamonds.* Forcing, showing 11–15 high-card points and at least four-card support.

7] *One notrump.* Shows 8–10 points and a balanced hand and denies a four-card or longer major suit.

8] *Two hearts.* A typical jump shift response.

9] *Pass.* You don't have to worry about "keeping the bidding open" after a *limited* Precision opening bid and should usually pass with 0–7 points.

10] *One spade.* Unless partner raises spades, you will *jump* in hearts on your next turn to insist upon reaching game.

11] *Three notrump.* Shows 14–15 points, a balanced hand, and no four-card or longer major suit.

12] *Three diamonds.* An ideal preemptive signoff.

13] *Two notrump.* Shows 16 or more high-card points and no good five-card or longer suit.

14] *Two clubs.* Shows at least 11 points and a good suit, and usually denies a four-card major suit.

15] *One notrump.* A 2 ♡ rebid would show a maximum.

16] *Two spades.* Show stoppers after a 2 ♣ response, just as you would after a raise to 2 ◊.

17] *One spade.* Shows a minimum with a four-card or longer spade suit.

18] *Two diamonds.* Shows a minimum with a six-card or longer diamond suit, and denies four-card or longer spade support.

19] *Three notrump.* Shows a maximum with stoppers in both major suits.

20] *Three hearts.* Jump to show a maximum with four-card or longer support.

21] *Three hearts.* Shows a maximum, a stopper in hearts, and no spade stopper.

22] *Two spades.* Jump to show a maximum 1 ◊ opening bid.

23] *Three clubs.* Shows a maximum with no stopper in either major.

24] *One notrump.* A 2 ♣ rebid would show a more unbalanced hand.

25] *Two notrump.* Shows a minimum with stoppers in both major suits.

9

Auctions
after a 2♣ opening bid

The 2♣ opening bid

A PRECISION 2 ♣ OPENING BID shows 11–15 points and a *good* five-card or longer club suit. If you have only five clubs, you must also have a side four-card *major* suit in order to open with 2 ♣. Let's look at some examples which will help to clarify these requirements:

> ♠ 6   ♡ A 7 6 4   ◇ K 10 4   ♣ A Q J 9 6:
> *Open* 2 ♣. You have 14 points, a good five-card club suit, and a side four-card major.

> ♠ A 8 5   ♡ 7   ◇ 9 7 6   ♣ A K J 7 4 3:
> *Open* 2 ♣. Your excellent six-card suit clearly warrants the two-level opening bid.

> ♠ A 7 3   ♡ 6 2   ◇ K 8 3   ♣ A Q J 8 4:
> *Open* 1 NT. With 5-3-3-2 distribution and 13–15 points, and the five-card suit a *minor*, prefer the highly descriptive 1 NT opening bid.

> ♠ 8 7   ♡ A 6   ◇ Q 10 3 2   ♣ A K 6 4 2:
> *Open* 1 ◇. With only five clubs and no side four-card major, leave room to explore for the best contract.

> ♠ K 7   ♡ A Q 7 6   ◇ 6 2   ♣ Q 8 6 4 2:
> *Pass.* The clubs are too weak to bid at the two-level, and a 1 ♡ opening bid would promise a five-card suit.

Non-forcing responses to a 2♣ opening bid

If your partner opens the bidding with 2 ♣, you should usually pass with 0–7 high-card points. Game is out of the question, and looking around for a better part score could easily result in a catastrophe that would keep the opponents happy for months.

With 8 or more points, one of the following non-forcing responses may be just what you need:

> 2 ♡ or 2 ♠ = 8–10 high-card points and a five-card or longer suit. With a minimum (11–13 high-card points), opener should pass with a tolerance for your suit and sign off in 3 ♣ if he views your suit with extreme distaste. With a maximum (14–15 high-card points), opener may invite game by raising your suit with three-card or longer support, or by bidding 2 NT.

> 3 ♣ = 8–10 high-card points, good three-card or better club support, and no five-card or longer major suit. Opener should pass with a minimum and bid 3 NT or a new suit with a maximum.

> 2 NT = 11–12 high-card points and a balanced hand with no four-card or longer major suit. Opener should pass with a balanced minimum, sign off in 3 ♣ with an unbalanced minimum and a six-card or longer club suit, and bid 3 NT or a new suit with a maximum.

Some examples of these responses to a 2 ♣ opening bid:

> ♠ Q 8 6 4 3   ♡ Q 4 2   ◊ J 3 2   ♣ 8 6:
> *Pass.* Don't try for a better part score with a weak hand unless you have made a side bet on the opponents!

> ♠ 8 7 2   ♡ A Q 10 6 2   ◊ K J 3   ♣ 7 4:
> *Bid* 2 ♡, showing a five-card or longer suit and 8–10

high-card points. Pass if partner signs off in 3 ♣, but accept any game invitation (such as a 3 ♡ or 2 NT rebid).

♠ A Q J 8 7 4   ♡ 7 4 3   ◊ 10 8 7 4   ♣ ——:
Bid 2 ♠. You have only 7 high-card points, but your excellent spade suit (and the hideous club void) warrant the 2 ♠ response. Refuse any game invitation.

♠ 6 4   ♡ A J 8   ◊ K 7 6 3   ♣ J 10 6 5:
Raise to 3 ♣ to show 8–10 high-card points and good club support.

♠ K 9 8   ♡ K 10 7   ◊ A J 8 6   ♣ 4 3 2:
Bid 2 NT, showing 11–12 high-card points and a balanced hand with no four-card or longer major suit.

Strong responses to a 2♣ opening bid

Jump shifts by responder

After a 2 ♣ opening bid by partner, jump in a good new five-card or longer suit if you have at least 14 high-card points (enough to justify reaching game even if opener has an 11-point minimum). For example, if partner opens with 2 ♣, respond as follows:

♠ 7 6   ♡ A K J 6 4   ◊ A K 10 5   ♣ Q 2:
Jump to 3 ♡.

♠ A K Q 10 8 5   ♡ 7 2   ◊ A J 4   ♣ 6 5:
Jump to 3 ♠.

After a jump shift, opener should rebid 3 NT with poor support for responder's suit. With three-card or longer support, opener should make a single raise with a minimum (11–13 high-card points) and cue-bid his cheapest ace with a maximum (14–15 high-card points).

The 2 ◊ convention

After a 2 ♣ opening bid, a 2 ◊ response is conventional and forcing; it promises at least 11 high-card points and asks opener to provide a further description of his hand.* Opener complies by rebidding as follows:

2 ♡ or 2 ♠ = four-card (or longer) suit, 11–13 high-card points.

2 NT = six-card club suit, stoppers in *two* of the three side suits, 11–13 high-card points.

3 ♣ = six-card club suit, *one* side suit stopped, 11–13 high-card points.

3 ◊ = minor two-suiter with at least six clubs and five diamonds.

3 ♡ or 3 ♠ = four-card (or longer) suit, 14–15 high-card points.

3 NT = solid six-card club suit, 14–15 high-card points.

4 ♣ = long, broken club suit, 14–15 high-card points.

These rebids will often limit opener's hand so sharply that responder will be able to place the contract on his next turn. In some cases, however, responder may need more information:

1] If opener rebids 2 NT, responder can bid 3 ◊ (conventional) to find out which two side suits opener has stopped. Opener answers as follows:

> 3 ♡ = hearts and diamonds stopped
> 3 ♠ = spades and diamonds stopped
> 3 NT = hearts and spades stopped

* With a good club fit, the high-card point requirement may be lowered to 8.

2] If opener rebids 3 ♣, showing only one side-suit stopper, responder can bid 3 ◇ (conventional) to find out where it is. Opener answers as follows:

> 3 ♡ = heart stopper
> 3 ♠ = spade stopper
> 3 NT = diamond stopper

Let's look at some examples of the 2 ◇ convention in action:

Opener	Responder	Opener	Responder
♠ A 8 5	♠ 6 3 2	2 ♣	2 ◇
♡ 7	♡ A J 9 2	3 ♣	3 ◇
◇ 9 7 6	◇ A Q 8	3 ♠	3 NT
♣ A K J 7 4 3	♣ Q 6 2	Pass	

After the 2 ♣ opening bid, responder needs more information in order to decide whether clubs, hearts, or notrump will be the best contract. He therefore puts the 2 ◇ convention into operation, and opener's rebid shows a six-card club suit and one side-suit stopper. Responder's spade doubleton is leering at him menacingly, so he bids 3 ◇ to find out just where opener's stopper is; upon hearing that it is in spades, he readily contracts for the notrump game. (Had opener's stopper been in a red suit, responder would have returned to 4 ♣.)

Opener	Responder	Opener	Responder
♠ K 7	♠ A Q 8 3	2 ♣	2 ◇
♡ A J 8 3	♡ K Q 6 5	2 ♡	4 ♡
◇ 8	◇ K 9 4	Pass	
♣ K J 10 8 6 4	♣ 9 5		

In this example, the 2 ◇ convention enables responder to locate the 4-4 heart fit, and he has enough strength to raise to game even though opener has shown a minimum.

Opener	Responder	Opener	Responder
♠ K J 3	♠ 6 5 2	2 ♣	2 ◇
♡ K J 6	♡ 10 4 2	2 NT	3 ◇
◇ 2	◇ A K J 3	3 NT	Pass
♣ K J 10 8 7 4	♣ A Q 6		

Opener's rebid of 2 NT shows a six-card club suit and stoppers in two side suits, and responder is keenly interested in where those stoppers are. He bids 3 ◊ to find out, and opener's 3 NT rebid reveals that his stoppers are in spades and hearts—just where responder needs them.

Opener	Responder	Opener	Responder
♠ K J 3	♠ A Q 4	2 ♣	2 ◊
♡ K J 6	♡ 10 5 3	2 NT	3 ◊
◊ 2	◊ 7 6 3	3 NT	4 ♣
♣ K J 10 8 7 4	♣ A Q 6 5	Pass	

This time, responder is hoping that opener will rebid 3 ♡ over 2 NT, showing stoppers in the red suits. When opener unobligingly rebids 3 NT, responder cleverly discerns that the diamond suit is a potential source of disaster in a notrump contract and properly returns to 4 ♣.

Opener	Responder	Opener	Responder
♠ 5 3	♠ Q J 10 4	2 ♣	2 ◊
♡ A K J 3	♡ 9 8	3 ♡	3 NT
◊ 6 2	◊ A J 9	Pass	
♣ A Q 8 6 4	♣ K 7 3 2		

With only 11 high-card points, responder plans to play in a part score if opener shows a minimum. When opener jumps to 3 ♡, indicating a four-card (or longer) heart suit and a maximum, responder correctly goes on to 3 NT.

When the opponents interfere

If a 2 ♣ opening bid is followed by a takeout double, a re-double promises at least 11 high-card points and strength in all unbid suits. It strongly suggests that the surest road to a large profit is to make a penalty double of a contract bid by the opponents. Other responses, including the 2 ◊ convention, retain the usual meaning.

If a 2 ♣ opening bid is followed by an overcall, a double at the three-level or higher is for penalties; a double at the two-level is negative and asks opener to bid a four-card (or longer) major suit if he has one. If the overcall has been at the two-level, a 2 NT response takes the place of the 2 ◊ convention. Opener rebids 3 ♣ with *any* minimum hand (11–13 high-card points) ; otherwise, his rebids retain the usual meaning.*

* A cue-bid of the enemy suit at the three-level shows at least one stopper, and not necessarily a four-card suit.

Auctions after a 2♣ opening bid

Opening bid of 2 ♣ = 11–15 points, at least five *good* clubs. With only five cards in clubs, hand must include a four-card *major* suit.

Responder's bid	*Opener's rebid*

Pass = 0–7 points.

2 ◊ = conventional, forcing. At least 11 high-card points; asks opener to describe his hand.

2 ♡ or 2 ♠ = four-card (or longer) suit, 11–13 high-card points.

2 NT = six-card club suit, stoppers in *two* of the three side suits, 11–13 high-card points. Responder may now bid 3 ◊ to ask where the stoppers are, and opener answers as follows:

    3 ♡ = hearts and diamonds stopped.

    3 ♠ = spades and diamonds stopped.

    3 NT = spades and hearts stopped.

3 ♣ = six-card club suit, *one* side suit stopped, 11–13 high-card points. Responder may now bid 3 ◊ to ask where the stopper is, and opener answers as follows:

    3 ♡ = hearts stopped.

    3 ♠ = spades stopped.

    3 NT = diamonds stopped.

3 ◊ = minor two-suiter (at least 6–5).

Responder's bid	*Opener's rebid*
	3 ♡ or 3 ♠ = four-card (or longer) suit, 14–15 high-card points.
	3 NT = solid six-card club suit, 14–15 high-card points.
	4 ♣ = long, broken club suit, 14–15 high-card points.
2 ♡ or 2 ♠ = 8–10 high-card points, five-card or longer suit. Not forcing.	3 ♣ = signoff.
	Single raise = invitation to game, three-card or longer support.
	2 NT = invitation to game, poor support.
2 NT = 11–12 high-card points, balanced hand with no four-card or longer major suit. Not forcing.	3 ♣ = signoff.
	New suit = maximum, forcing.
	3 NT = maximum, signoff.
3 ♣ = 8–10 high-card points, good three-card or better club support. No five-card or longer major suit. Not forcing.	New suit = maximum, forcing.
	3 NT = maximum, signoff.
Jump shift = 14 or more high-card points, good five-card or longer suit. Forcing to game.	3 NT = any hand with poor support (0–2 cards) for responder's suit.
	Single raise = three-card or longer support; minimum hand.
	New suit = maximum hand, three-card or longer support, ace in bid suit.

REVIEW QUIZ

PART I.
In each of the following problems, what is your opening bid?

1] ♠ A Q 8 6
♡ 10 6 3
◇ 7
♣ K Q J 9 5

2] ♠ K J 7 4
♡ Q 3
◇ Q 4
♣ K 8 6 4 3

3] ♠ K 3
♡ Q 10 3
◇ K 8 7
♣ A Q J 8 7

4] ♠ K Q 5 3 2
♡ 7
◇ A
♣ K J 8 6 4 3

5] ♠ A K
♡ 8 7
◇ A J 8 6
♣ Q 10 7 5 2

PART II.
In each of the following problems, partner opens the bidding with 2 ♣. What is your response?

6] ♠ A 6 4
♡ 7 2
◇ K 8 3 2
♣ Q 10 8 4

7] ♠ A Q 8 6 5
♡ 7 3
◇ A Q 3
♣ 5 3 2

8] ♠ K Q 10 8 6 2
♡ 7
◇ A 5 3
♣ 6 4 2

9] ♠ A 9 8
♡ K Q J 5 2
◇ A Q 3
♣ 6 2

10] ♠ Q 6 3
♡ K 10 8 7 4
◇ 8 6 2
♣ 9 5

11] ♠ K Q 8 2
♡ A 9 7 3
◇ 8 6 2
♣ K 3

12] ♠ K 8 3
♡ A Q 7
◇ J 10 8 6
♣ Q 3 2

PART III.
In each of the following problems, you have opened with 2 ♣ and partner has responded 2 ◇. What is your rebid?

13] ♠ 2
♡ K Q 3
◇ A 10 7
♣ Q 10 9 8 3 2

14] ♠ Q 10 4 2
♡ K 8 3
◇ 7
♣ A Q J 6 2

15] ♠ A K J 3
♡ 6
◇ 5 2
♣ A Q 10 8 6 5

Solutions

1] *Two clubs.* Your hand meets all the requirements: 12 high-card points, and a good five-card club suit with a side four-card major.

2] *Pass.* The clubs are too weak to bid at the two level. Also, the unprotected red-suit honors strongly suggest a conservative course.

3] *One notrump.* The best choice with 5-3-3-2 distribution and 13-15 high-card points when your five-card suit is a minor.

4] *Two clubs.* With a two-suiter, start with your longer suit.

5] *One diamond.* There are two excellent reasons for avoiding the 2 ♣ opening bid: The clubs are too weak, and you don't have a four-card major to go along with your five-card club suit.

6] *Three clubs.* Shows 8-10 high-card points and good club support.

7] *Two diamonds.* A 2 ♠ response would show 8-10 high-card points, and a 3 ♠ response would promise at least 14 high-card points.

8] *Two spades.* Shows 8-10 high-card points and at least five spades.

9] *Three hearts.* Jump shift with 14 or more high-card points and a good five-card or longer suit.

10] *Pass.* Don't go looking for trouble with weak hands!

11] *Two diamonds.* You need more information—for example, whether or not opener has a four-card major suit and whether he has a minimum or a maximum.

12] *Two notrump.* Shows 11-12 high-card points and a balanced hand with no four-card major suit.

13] *Two notrump.* Shows a minimum with a six-card club suit and stoppers in two side suits. If partner now bids 3 ◊, respond 3 ♡ to show stoppers in hearts and diamonds.

14] *Two spades.* Shows a minimum with a four-card spade suit.

15] *Three spades.* Jump to show a maximum.

10

Auctions
after a 2♦opening bid

The 2♦ opening bid

A PRECISION 2 ◊ OPENING BID shows 11–15 points and 4-4-1-4 or 4-4-0-5 distribution with shortness in *diamonds*. Let's examine the uses of this important conventional opening bid by looking at some examples:

> ♠ A Q 7 6   ♡ K 9 7 4   ◊ 7   ♣ A J 6 3:
>
> *Open* 2 ◊. As we saw in Chapter 1, you certainly should open the bidding with this 14-point hand. However, you can't bid a four-card major suit, your unbalanced suit distribution rules out a 1 NT opening bid, and a 1 ♣ opening bid would promise at least 16 points. Therefore, a conventional 2 ◊ opening bid is used for hands such as this one.

> ♠ K J 8 6   ♡ Q 10 6 3   ◊ ——   ♣ A K 10 9 7:
>
> *Open* 2 ◊. Although the clubs are strong enough for a 2 ♣ opening bid, the 2 ◊ call is much more descriptive; you can inform partner about all three of your suits in a single bid.

The 2 ◊ opening bid is also essential when you have 4-3-1-5 distribution with shortness in diamonds, a *weak* five-card club suit, and 13-15 high-card points:

> ♠ A J 7   ♡ K Q 8 6   ◊ 6   ♣ K 8 6 4 2:
>
> *Open* 2 ◊. The clubs are too weak for a 2 ♣ opening bid, your hand doesn't meet the requirements for a

1 ♡ or 1 NT opening, and you have too much strength to pass.

However, do *not* open 2 ◊ with any of the following hands:

♠ K J 6 3   ♡ 10 8 2   ◊ 4   ♣ A K J 9 7:
Open 2 ♣. With 4-3-1-5 distribution, prefer the 2 ♣ opening bid when your club suit is strong.

♠ A Q 6   ♡ K Q 8 6   ◊ 6   ♣ 10 9 7 4 2:
Pass. With only 11–12 points, refuse to compromise; don't open 2 ◊ unless you have 4-4-1-4 or 4-4-0-5 distribution.

♠ A Q 8 6   ♡ A 7   ◊ K 6   ♣ Q 10 7 4 2:
Open 1 NT. The clubs are too weak to bid at the two-level, the distribution is unsuitable for a 2 ◊ opening bid, and the hand is too good for a pass. The weak notrump is a reasonable solution in spite of the somewhat unbalanced distribution.

♠ A Q 8 6   ♡ 7   ◊ A K 3   ♣ J 9 7 3 2:
Open 1 ◊. Here, the best compromise is to bid the strong three-card diamond suit; the distribution is too unbalanced for a 1 NT opening bid.

♠ K Q 8 6   ♡ A 7   ◊ Q 5   ♣ J 6 4 3 2:
Pass. No reasonable opening bid is available—and this is certainly no hardship in view of your meager assets.

Non-forcing responses to a 2♠ opening bid

If partner opens with 2 ◊, keep in mind that he has at most a singleton diamond. If you pass with two or three small diamonds just because you have a weak hand, you may well wind up searching for a new partner after the hand is over!

Pass only with *six* or more diamonds and 0–10 high-card points.

With 0–7 high-card points and fewer than six diamonds, take advantage of the fact that partner must have fine support for the other three suits by signing off in the one you like best.* Since you have found your best denomination in a single bid, you are unlikely to be in serious trouble even though your hand is weak.

As illustrations, let us suppose that partner has opened with 2 ◊ and you hold each of the following hands. What call do you make?

♠ 8 6   ♡ Q 3 2   ◊ Q J 10 8 4 3   ♣ 6 2:
Pass. Your diamonds can withstand partner's singleton or void, and there is nowhere else to go.

♠ K 6   ♡ 7 3 2   ◊ A Q 7 6 4 3   ♣ 3 2:
Pass. Thanks to the Precision 2 ◊ opening, you have discovered a bad misfit early enough to stay out of serious trouble—provided that you don't let your 9 high-card points entice you into doing something silly. Your side has no satisfactory trump suit and at most 24 high-card points.

♠ 10 8 7 2   ♡ 6 2   ◊ 8 6 4 3   ♣ 4 3 2:
Bid 2 ♠. Partner must pass.

♠ Q 8 3   ♡ J 7 2   ◊ 6 4 3   ♣ J 10 8 7:
Sign off in 3 ♣.

♠ 8 7 6   ♡ Q 8 6 4 2   ◊ Q 3 2   ♣ 10 7:
Sign off in 2 ♡.

After a 2 ◊ opening bid, a raise to 3 ◊ is not forcing and shows 11–13 high-card points and a semi-solid six-card or longer

---

* You may wish to use a jump to 3 ♡ or 3 ♠ to show a good five-card or longer suit and 5-7 high-card points with no wasted values in diamonds, asking opener to raise to game if he has 14-15 high-card points and can add 5 distribution points for a void in diamonds when raising your suit.

diamond suit. Opener is requested to bid 3 NT with 14–15 high-card points and to pass otherwise. For example, raise a 2 ◊ opening bid to 3 ◊ with

     ♠ K 10 3   ♡ 8 7   ◊ A Q J 10 6 2   ♣ Q 5

If your diamond suit is completely solid and you have 11–13 high-card points, jump to 3 NT yourself:

     ♠ K 10 3   ♡ 8 7   ◊ A K Q J 6 2   ♣ 4 3:
     If partner opens with 2 ◊, jump to 3 NT.

Forcing response to a 2♠ opening bid: The 2 NT convention

The only forcing response that you can make after a 2 ◊ opening bid is 2 NT. This bid is conventional, shows 8 or more high-card points, and asks opener to further describe his hand. Opener obliges by rebidding as follows:

    3 ♣ = 3-4-1-5 distribution with 4-card heart suit. If responder wants to know opener's point count range, he can bid 3 ◊ (conventional); opener rebids 3 ♡ with 11–13 high-card points and 3 ♠ with 14–15 high-card points.

    3 ◊ = 4-3-1-5 distribution with 4-card spade suit. Responder may now use 3 ♡ (conventional) to ask about opener's point count range, and opener rebids 3 ♠ with 11–13 high-card points and 3 NT with 14–15 high-card points.

    3 ♡ = 11–13 high-card points, 4-4-1-4 distribution.

    3 ♠ = 14–15 high-card points, 4-4-1-4 distribution.

    3 NT = 14–15 high-card points, 4-4-1-4 distribution with singleton ace or king of diamonds.

4 ♣ = 11–13 high-card points, 4-4-0-5 distribution.

4 ◇ = 14–15 high-card points, 4-4-0-5 distribution.

The 2 NT convention will help you answer the following important questions:

1] Does opener have a minimum or maximum? Do we have game or slam?

2] What denomination should we play in? Do we have a 4–4 major fit, or is a notrump or club contract better?

Let's look at some examples:

Opener	Responder		Opener	Responder
♠ A J 7	♠ K 10 6 4		2 ◇	2 NT
♡ K Q 8 6	♡ A J 3		3 ♣	3 NT
◇ 6	◇ A Q 9 7		Pass	
♣ K 8 6 4 2	♣ 7 5			

Responder has enough points to insist upon reaching game, and wishes to know whether to play in 3 NT or 4 ♠. When opener rebids 3 ♣, showing 3-4-1-5 distribution and a 4 card heart suit, responder selects 3 NT as the final contract.

Opener	Responder		Opener	Responder
♠ A Q 8 6	♠ K J 10 9 2		2 ◇	2 NT
♡ Q J 7 2	♡ A K 6		4 ◇	4 NT
◇ ——	◇ 9 7 6 3		5 ◇	6 ♠
♣ K Q 6 3 2	♣ 4		Pass	

As it happens, opener bids diamonds three times with his void! His rebid of 4 ◇ shows 14–15 high-card points and 4-4-0-5 distribution. Responder keenly observes that he has no wasted values in diamonds opposite opener's void, and decides to try for slam by using Blackwood. When opener shows one ace, responder contracts for 6 ♠—reaching a virtually laydown slam with a combined holding of 25 high-card points.

Auctions after a 2♦ opening bid

Opening bid of 2 ♦ = 11–15 high-card points and 4-4-1-4 or 4-4-0-5 distribution with shortness in *diamonds,* or 13–15 high-card points and 4-3-1-5 distribution with a four-card major suit and shortness in diamonds.

Responder's bid	*Opener's rebid*
Pass = 0–10 high-card points, at least *six* diamonds.	
2 ♡, 2 ♠, or 3 ♣ = signoff, 0–7 high-card points.	
2 NT = conventional, forcing. 8 or more high-card points, asks opener to describe his hand.	3 ♣ = 4-3-1-5 distribution with 4-card heart suit. Responder can now bid 3 ♦ to ask for point count range, and opener answers as follows: 3 ♡ = 11–13 high-card points 3 ♠ = 14–15 high-card points 3 ♦ = 4-3-1-5 distribution with 4-card spade suit. Responder can now use 3 ♡ to ask for point-count range, and opener answers as follows: 3 ♠ = 11–13 high-card points 3 NT = 14–15 high-card points

Responder's bid	*Opener's rebid*
	3 ♡ = 11–13 high-card points, 4-4-1-4 distribution.
	3 ♠ = 14–15 high-card points, 4-4-1-4 distribution.
	3 NT = 14–15 high-card points, 4-4-1-4 distribution with singleton ace or king of diamonds.
	4 ♣ = 11–13 high-card points, 4-4-0-5 distribution.
	4 ◊ = 14–15 high-card points, 4-4-0-5 distribution.
3 ◊ = 11–13 high-card points, semi-solid six-card diamond suit. Not forcing.	Pass = 11–13 high-card points. 3 NT = 14–15 high-card points.
3 NT = 11–13 high-card points, solid six-card diamond suit. Signoff.	

REVIEW QUIZ

PART I.

What is your opening bid in each of the following problems?

1] ♠ K 8 6 3   2] ♠ K Q 7 3   3] ♠ K 6 3 2   4] ♠ K Q 7
   ♡ Q J 7 2   ♡ A K 3   ♡ A Q 8 5   ♡ A 9 7 3
   ◇ 6   ◇ 6   ◇ --   ◇ 2
   ♣ A Q 10 2   ♣ Q 10 8 3 2   ♣ A Q 6 3 2   ♣ K Q J 10 6

5] ♠ A J 8 6   6] ♠ K 10 7   7] ♠ K 3
   ♡ Q   ♡ K Q 3 2   ♡ K J 9 5
   ◇ K J 3   ◇ 7   ◇ A 10
   ♣ J 6 5 4 2   ♣ K 9 7 6 4   ♣ K 6 4 3 2

PART II.

Partner has opened the bidding with 2 ◇ in each of the following problems. What is your response?

8] ♣ K 10   9] ♠ 6 4 2   10] ♠ 8 6 2
   ♡ 7 2   ♡ Q 3   ♡ Q 4
   ◇ A Q J 10 9 6 ◇ 7 5 4 3   ◇ A Q 10 9 6 5
   ♣ J 10 7   ♣ 10 9 8 7   ♣ 7 3

11] ♠ K Q 6 3   12] ♠ K 10 6 4
    ♡ 7 2   ♡ J 3
    ◇ A K 3   ◇ Q 8 6 3 2
    ♣ 10 9 7 4   ♣ 7 2

PART III.

You have opened with 2 ◇ and partner has responded 2 NT in each of the following problems. What is your rebid?

13] ♠ K Q 8   14] ♠ K 8 6 3   15] ♠ A J 8 3
    ♡ A Q 6 5   ♡ Q 10 5 2   ♡ K J 10 9
    ◇ 7   ◇ --   ◇ J
    ♣ A 7 5 3 2   ♣ A Q J 6 3   ♣ K 10 8 2

Solutions

1] *Two diamonds.* Your hand meets all the requirements.

2] *Two diamonds.* The clubs are too weak for a 2 ♣ opening bid, and your hand is too strong to pass.

3] *Two diamonds.* An ideal hand for the 2 ◊ opening bid.

4] *Two clubs.* A better choice than 2 ◊ with 4–3–1–5 distribution when the clubs are strong.

5] *Pass.* You have meager values and no good bid to make.

6] *Pass.* Don't open 2 ◊ with 4–3–1–5 distribution unless you have a good reason—namely, 13–15 high-card points.

7] *One notrump.* Not ideal with relatively unbalanced distribution, but the only possible choice. You would like to open with 2 ♣, but the clubs are not strong enough.

8] *Three diamonds.* Shows a semi-solid diamond suit and 11–13 high-card points, and invites partner to bid 3 NT with a maximum.

9] *Three clubs.* Don't pass in disgust! You are certain to improve the contract by bidding 3 ♣.

10] *Pass.* Your side has a misfit, so there is no reason to proceed further.

11] *Two notrump.* You need more information to decide whether or not your side has game, and what denomination will be best.

12] *Two spades.* Sign off in what is certain to be the best contract.

13] *Three clubs.* Shows 4–3–1–5 distribution with a four-card heart suit.

14] *Four clubs.* Shows 11–13 high-card points and 4–4–0–5 distribution.

15] *Three hearts.* Shows 11–13 high-card points and 4–4–1–4 distribution.

11

Other opening bids and responses

Preemptive bids

PRECISION OPENING BIDS of three or four of a suit are standard preemptives, showing a long and strong suit with little of value on the side. These preempts will usually prove very infuriating to the opponents by disrupting their normal channels of bidding. To minimize the chance that they will infuriate you by saying "double" and subsequently writing down a large number on their side of the score sheet, be within three tricks of your bid if you are not vulnerable and two tricks if you are vulnerable:

♠ 7 3   ♡ K Q J 10 9 7 5   ◇ 6 3 2   ♣ 4:
Open 3 ♡ if you are not vulnerable.*

♠ A Q 10 9 8 0 5 3   ♡ 7 3   ◇ 6   ♣ 4 2:
With reasonable luck, you will win seven spade tricks. *Open* 4 ♠ not vulnerable and 3 ♠ vulnerable.

♠ 7   ♡ 6 3   ◇ A K Q 9 8 4 3 2   ♣ J 7:
Open 5 ◇ not vulnerable and 4 ◇ vulnerable.

♠ J 9 7 6 4 3 2   ♡ A 6 3   ◇ 6 2   ♣ 4:
Pass. Your suit is too weak for a preempt.

♠ A 7   ♡ K Q J 10 9 7 3   ◇ K 6   ♣ 6 2:
Open 1 ♡. You have too much side strength for a preempt.

---

* If you are vulnerable, it is reasonable to promote this hand because of the solid suit and open with 2 ♡ (see next section).

After a preemptive opening bid, responder can usually place the contract immediately. For example, suppose that partner opens with a non-vulnerable 3 ♡ bid and you hold one of the following hands:

♠ A J 8 7 6 2   ♡ 7   ◇ K 6 3   ♣ 8 5 2:
   Pass. Game is out of reach, and partner has promised a good heart suit.

♠ A 8 6 2   ♡ 4   ◇ A K 5 3   ♣ A 10 3 2:
   Raise to 4 ♡. Partner has promised six tricks, and you can supply four more. Opener is very short of side entries, so don't bid notrump with a poor fit for his suit.

A preemptive opening tells the full story of your hand in a single bid. Don't succumb to the sad fate that befalls many preempters who become mesmerized by the playing strength of their long suit:

South	West	North	East
3 ♡	3 ♠	4 ♡	4 ♠
5 ♡???	Double	*!#†‡	

North holds four sure defensive tricks and is ready to chalk up a profit, but South foolishly tells the same story twice by bidding again and hands the plus score to East-West. The moral: *After you have made a preemptive opening bid, partner is in charge of all subsequent decisions.* He knows exactly what you have, and you *don't* know what he has!

Weak two-bids

Precision opening bids of 2 ♡ and 2 ♠ are preemptive and show 8–10 high-card points and a *good* six-card suit. Some examples:

♠ A Q J 8 6 3   ♡ Q 3 2   ◇ 8 6 3   ♣ 10:
   Open 2 ♠. Your hand has fine offensive potential and

is poorly suited for defense. Since it is not strong enough for a three-level preempt, the weak two-bid is the ideal solution.

♠ 6 2   ♡ A J 10 9 7 2   ◊ K 7 3   ♣ 4 2:
Open 2 ♡.

♠ K 8 3   ♡ J 8 7 6 4 2   ◊ A 7   ♣ 6 3:
Pass. A weak two-bid shows a good suit and poor defensive strength—exactly the opposite of what you have!

After a weak two-bid, any game bid by responder is a signoff, and a raise of opener's suit is also a signoff. A simple new suit response is natural and forcing; opener should raise with three-card or longer support and rebid his suit with poor support. Precision uses a 2 NT response to ask opener to show a singleton or void if he has one and rebid his suit if he does not; this convention can be useful in exploring game or slam possibilities when responder has a powerful hand. Let's look at a few examples:

Opener	Responder
2 ♠	?

♠ A 7   ♡ A K 7 6   ◊ 7 6 3   ♣ A Q 5 2:
Raise to 4 ♠. Partner has promised a good six-card suit, so a doubleton honor is sufficient support.

♠ Q 8 6 4   ♡ 7   ◊ K Q J 9 7 4   ♣ 7 3:
Raise to 4 ♠. The opponents can probably make game in hearts. If they think you are bidding on high-card strength, they might give up and pass; if they double, you have enough playing strength to guard against a serious penalty.

♠ 7   ♡ A J 8 4   ◊ K 10 6   ♣ Q J 7 4 2:
Pass. Game is out of reach, so don't court disaster by bidding further.

♠ 7   ♡ A Q J 6 3   ◇ A K 4   ♣ Q J 10 3:
Bid 3 ♡. Partner will raise to 4 ♡ with three-card support; if instead he returns to 3 ♠, bid 3 NT.

The 2 NT opening bid

A Precision 2 NT opening bid shows 22–23 high-card points and balanced suit distribution. For example, open 2 NT with

♠ A Q 6
♡ K Q 8 3
◇ A Q 10 7
♣ A Q

Precision recommends the following responses:

Pass = 0–3 high-card points, relatively balanced hand.
3 ♣ = Stayman. At least 3 high-card points.
3 ◇ = Jacoby transfer to 3 ♡ with five-card or longer heart suit. Responder may be planning to pass with a weak hand, bid 3 NT to offer opener a choice of games, bid 4 ♡ with a six-card or longer suit, or cue-bid a new suit to try for slam.
3 ♡ = Jacoby transfer to 3 ♠ with five-card or longer spade suit.
3 NT = signoff. At least 4 high-card points; balanced hand with no four-card or longer major suit.
4 ♣ = Gerber ace-asking convention.
4 NT ~ non-forcing; invitational to 6 NT. 10 high-card points, balanced hand with no four-card or longer major suit.

Some examples of responses to a 2 NT opening bid:

♠ 7 6 3   ♡ 2   ◇ 8 4 3 2   ♣ J 9 8 6 2:
Pass.

♠ J 9 8 6 2   ♡ 2   ◇ 7 6 3   ♣ 10 7 4 2:
> *Bid* 3 ♡ and pass partner's forced 3 ♠ response. The spades may well be worthless in a notrump contract.

♠ 7 3   ♡ A Q 10 6 2   ◇ Q 8 3   ♣ 6 4 2:
> *Bid* 3 ◇ and follow with 3 NT over partner's forced 3 ♡ response. He will pass with a doubleton heart and return to 4 ♡ with three-card or longer heart support.

♠ K 10 8   ♡ Q 7 2   ◇ 6 4 3   ♣ 8 7 6 2:
> *Bid* 3 NT.

♠ K 10 8 2   ♡ Q 7 2   ◇ 6 4 3 2   ♣ 7 4:
> *Bid* 3 ♣. If partner shows a four-card spade suit by bidding 3 ♠, raise to 4 ♠; otherwise, play in 3 NT.

♠ K 10 8   ♡ Q 7 3   ◇ A J 10 7   ♣ 8 7 2:
> *Bid* 4 NT, inviting partner to bid 6 NT with a maximum.

♠ K 10 8   ♡ Q 7 3   ◇ A J 10 7   ♣ Q 10 3:
> *Bid* 6 NT.

The 3 NT opening bid

You could probably agree with your partner never to open 3 NT without hurting your prospects at the bridge table. If you do wish to make use of this opening bid, there are two possibilities:

Alternative 1.   3 NT = 27–29 high-card points and balanced suit distribution. Such hands do occur once every few years or so, and are very difficult to handle by any other method.

Alternative 2.   3 NT = *solid* seven-card or eight-card *minor* suit and at most a queen on the side. The idea of this "gambling" 3 NT opening bid is to try and "steal" game by running nine tricks before the opponents can figure out what to do. If you select this method, use it only when not vulnerable.* Treat a 4 ♣ response as an "escape," asking opener to pass if clubs is his solid suit and bid 4 ◊ if his solid suit is in diamonds.

Other opening bids and responses

Opening bid	Response
2 ♡ or 2 ♠ = weak two-bid. 8–10 high-card points and good six-card suit.	2 NT = forcing, conventional. Asks opener to show a side-suit void or singleton if he has one and rebid his suit if he does not. New suit = forcing, natural. Opener should raise with three-card support and rebid his suit with poor support. Any raise or game bid = signoff.
2 NT = 22–23 high-card points, balanced suit distribution.	3 ♣ = Stayman. 3 ◇ = Jacoby transfer to 3 ♡. 3 ♡ = Jacoby transfer to 3 ♠. 3 NT = signoff. 4 ♣ = Gerber. 4 NT = non-forcing; invitational to 6 NT.
Three or four of a suit = standard preempt, showing long and strong suit with little side-suit strength. Opener is within three tricks of his bid if not vulnerable and two tricks if vulnerable.	Responder usually places the contract immediately.

REVIEW QUIZ

PART I.

Determine your opening bid in each of the following problems. Unless stated otherwise, you are not vulnerable.

1] ♠ K63
♡ KQJ873
◇ J72
♣ 4

2] ♠ AKQ
♡ KQ8
◇ KJ63
♣ A105

3] ♠ KQJ108732
♡ A63
◇ 7
♣ 5

(You are vulnerable)

4] ♠ Q86543
♡ A72
◇ 4
♣ K63

5] ♠ 73
♡ KQ109863
◇ Q62
♣ 7

6] ♠ AK3
♡ Q1087543
◇ K2
♣ 10

PART II.

Partner's opening bid is shown; determine your response in each of the following problems. Unless stated otherwise, you are not vulnerable.

7] *Opener's Bid 2 ♠*
♠ K86
♡ AKJ652
◇ K32
♣ 8

8] *Opener's Bid 2 NT*
♠ KQ86
♡ 9863
◇ J862
♣ 5

9] *Opener's Bid 3 ♡*
♠ AK63
♡ 7
◇ KQ97
♣ A962

10] *Opener's Bid 2 ♡*
♠ K862
♡ 7
◇ AQ86
♣ QJ32

11] *Opener's Bid 2 NT*
♠ Q86
♡ A83
◇ 74
♣ 97643

12] *Opener's Bid 4 ♠*
♠ 7
♡ A865
◇ A732
♣ K943

(You are vulnerable)

13] *Opener's Bid* 2 NT	14] *Opener's Bid* 2 ♡	15] *Opener's Bid* 2 NT
♠ 863	♠ KQ10865	♠ AJ8642
♡ 6542	♡ 7	♡ 732
◊ Q63	◊ KJ3	◊ Q6
♣ 842	♣ AK4	♣ 75

Solutions

1] *Two hearts.* An ideal weak two-bid.

2] *Two notrump.* Your hand meets all the requirements.

3] *Four spades.* You have eight tricks and an ideal hand for a preemptive opening bid. (Not vulnerable, you would also open with 4 ♠. To be sure, you are within three tricks of a 5 ♠ opening bid, but you will have great difficulty explaining the lost game bonus to partner if you do open with 5 ♠ and go down one. *Don't* preempt above the level of game!)

4] *Pass.* Your poor spades and substantial side-suit strength are good reasons to avoid a weak two-bid.

5] *Three hearts.* You can reasonably expect to take six heart tricks, so you are within three tricks of your non-vulnerable preempt.

6] *One heart.* You have too much side-suit strength for a preempt.

7] *Four spades.* Slam is beyond reach, and you have found a good trump suit. Don't help the opponents defend by bidding hearts.

8] *Three clubs.* Raise a major-suit rebid to game; bid 3 NT over a 3 ◊ rebid.

9] *Four hearts.* Don't bid 3 NT with a poor fit for opener's suit.

10] *Pass.* Game is out of reach, so stay out of trouble.

11] *Three notrump.* A good hand for the single raise.

12] *Pass.* Slam is unlikely opposite partner's eight-trick hand.

13] *Pass.* Not all roads lead to game after a 2 NT opening bid.

14] *Two spades.* You will rebid spades next time to force to game and offer partner a choice between 4 ♠ and 3 NT. Of course, if partner raises to 3 ♠, you can proceed directly to 4 ♠.

15] *Three hearts.* Partner is forced to bid 3 ♠, and you will raise to 4 ♠. Opener cannot have a void or singleton, so your side must have at least an eight-card spade fit.

12

Asking bids

The objectives of asking bids

SUPPOSE THAT YOU ARE FORTUNATE ENOUGH to deal yourself the following hand:

♠ Q J 6 2
♡ A K Q J 10 9
◇ 4 3
♣ A

You open the bidding with 1 ♣, and partner makes a positive response of 1 ♠. Slam is now a definite possibility, but there are important difficulties to overcome:

1]. Partner's spade suit may be weak. In a slam contract, no amount of side-suit strength can compensate for two trump losers!

2]. The diamond weakness may doom any slam contract to immediate defeat. Even if the combined partnership holdings in the other three suits are bristling with strength and length, a slam venture will prove quite humiliating if the opponents cash the first two diamond tricks.

The Blackwood convention is *not* likely to be an effective solution because you need information about specific suits—the trump suit (spades) and diamonds. Ideally, you would like to conduct a conversation such as the following one with your partner:

You: "Partner, we have a good spade fit and an excellent chance for slam. How strong is your spade suit?"

Partner: "I have five spades headed by the ace-king."

You: "Good! Slam prospects are improving rapidly. We're in danger of losing the first two tricks in diamonds; can you provide any help?"

Partner: "Yes. I have second-round control of diamonds ——either the king or a singleton."

You: "6 ♠."

If instead partner's second answer indicated possession of first-round diamond control (ace or void), you would bid 7 ♠; while if he told you that he could not prevent the loss of two diamond tricks, you would stop in 4 ♠. Of course, conversations such as this one are illegal; but it is perfectly legitimate to convey such messages by means of *asking bids*—conventional bids which ask partner to describe a specific aspect of his hand by means of conventional responses.* Several different asking bids are available to the Precision player, and we will consider each in turn.

The trump asking bid

The trump asking bid was presented in Chapter 5; for convenience, the responses are repeated in Table 2. As an illustration, let's return to the example of the preceding section:

	You	Partner
	1 ♣	1 ♠
	2 ♠	3 ◊

You hold: ♠ Q J 6 2   ♡ A K Q J 10 9   ◊ 4 3   ♣ A

Your 2 ♠ bid is the trump asking bid, agreeing on spades as the trump suit and asking partner (legally!) how good his spade suit is. Partner's 3 ◊ response is an upward move of three steps (2 NT = first step, 3 ♣ = second step), which shows five spades to two of the top three honors. Thus, you now know that your side has no trump losers. Slam is looming clearly on the horizon, but what about that troublesome diamond suit?

* Of course, an asking bid should be made in the same tone of voice as any other bid!

TABLE 2. Precison Asking Bids

1. *Trump asking bid*

Asking bid: Single raise of positive suit response to 1 ♣ opening bid.

Responses:	Steps above previous bid	Responder's suit length	Responder's suit strength
	1	5 or more cards	Jack-high or worse
	2	5 cards	1 of top 3 honors
	3	5 cards	2 of top 3 honors
	4	6 or more cards	1 of top 3 honors
	5	6 or more cards	2 of top 3 honors
	6	5 or more cards	All 3 top honors

2. *Control asking bid*

Asking bids: 1. New-suit bid by opener after answer to trump asking bid.
2. New-suit bid after answer to ace asking bid.

Responses:	Steps above previous bid	Controls in asked suit
	1	No control (three or more low cards)
	2	Third-round control (doubleton or Queen)
	3	Second-round control (singleton or King)
	4	First-round control (void or Ace)
	5	First-round and second-round control (AK or AQ)

3. *Ace asking bid*

Asking bid: Jump shift by 1 ♣ opener after any positive response.*

Responses:	Bid	Meaning ("Top Honor" = A, K, or Q)
	Cheapest NT	No top honor in asked suit; no side ace.
	Single raise	Top honor in asked suit; no side ace.
	New suit	No top honor in asked suit; ace in *bid* suit only.
	Jump new suit	Top honor in asked suit; ace in *bid* suit only.
	Jump in NT	No top honor in asked suit; two side aces.
	Jump raise	Top honor in asked suit; two side aces.

The control asking bid

After you have received the answer to your trump asking bid, the bid of any new suit is a *control asking bid* which asks partner to describe his strength in this suit. Responder's an-

---

* When using the ace asking bid, the 1 ♣ opener may jump shift in a six-card or longer suit that is only semi-solid (missing at most one top honor). He still must have at least 19 high-card points.

swers are defined in terms of steps (see Table 2); the more steps, the better the controls. In our example, the bidding should continue as follows:

You	Partner
1 ♣	1 ♠
2 ♠	3 ♦
4 ♦	

You hold: ♠ Q J 6 2   ♡ A K Q J 10 9   ◊ 4 3   ♣ A

Your 4 ◊ bid is the control asking bid, inquiring as to partner's ability to prevent a disaster in diamonds. Let's see how his possible replies will enable you to place the contract in a single bid:

Partner's answer	Your action
4 ♡	Sign off in 4 ♠. Partner has no controls in diamonds.
4 ♠	Pass. Partner's third-round control of diamonds won't prevent a debacle in a slam contract.
4 NT	Bid 6 ♠. Partner's king or singleton in diamonds will ensure the loss of no more than one trick.
5 ♣	Bid 7 ♠. Partner has the ace or void in diamonds.
5 ◊	Bid 7 NT. Partner must have the diamond ace and you can count thirteen top tricks, so bid the grand slam in notrump for maximum safety.

In some cases, more than one control asking bid may be necessary:

Opener	Responder
♠ K Q 3 2	♠ A 7
♡ A J 10 7	♡ K Q 8 6 4 2
◊ A K J 6 4	◊ 8 3
♣ ——	♣ 8 6 4

The bidding:

Opener	Responder
1 ♣	1 ♡
2 ♡¹	3 ♡²
3 ♠³	4 ♡⁴
5 ◇⁵	5 ♠⁶
7 ♡⁷	Pass

¹ "Hearts will be an ideal trump suit. Slam looks likely; how strong is your heart suit?"
² "It's a six-card or longer suit headed by two of the top three honors."
³ "Sounds good! How are you fixed for spade controls?"
⁴ "I've got first-round control."
⁵ "How about diamond controls?"
⁶ "Third-round control there."
⁷ "That's all I need to know!"

And a virtually laydown grand slam is reached with only 27 high-card points in the combined hands. Asking bids provide a unique feeling of power that is comparable to being able to see through the backs of your partner's cards—and there is nothing the opponents can do except suffer in silence.

The ace asking bid

After a 1 ♣ opening bid and a positive response, a jump shift rebid by opener may be treated as an *ace asking bid*. This asking bid *shows* at least a semi-solid six-card or longer suit (i.e., missing at most one of the top three honors) and 19 or more high-card points, and it *asks* partner to provide information about honors in opener's suit and side-suit aces. Responder's replies to this asking bid are *not* in terms of steps (see Table 2). After the answer to an ace asking bid, a bid in a new suit is a control asking bid.

Here's an example:

Opener	Responder
♠ A K J 9 7 6	♠ Q 8
♡ 7	♡ 10 8 6 4 2
◇ K Q J	◇ A 7 2
♣ A Q 3	♣ K 4 2

Opener	Responder
1 ♣	1 ♡
2 ♠¹	4 ◇²
5 ♣³	5 ♠⁴
6 ♠⁵	Pass

¹ Shows 19 or more high-card points and at least a semi-solid six-card or longer spade suit, and serves as an ace asking bid. Opener's battle plan is as follows: If responder bids 2 NT, showing no top spade honor and no side ace, opener will bid 3 NT to offer responder a choice of games. If responder bids 3 ♠, showing a top spade honor and no side ace, opener will sign off in 4 ♠. Otherwise, opener will try for slam.

² Responder jumps in a new suit to show a top honor in opener's suit, the ace in the bid suit, and no other side ace.

³ A control asking bid. Opener now knows that responder has the spade queen and diamond ace, and he keenly discerns that slam will be cold if responder also has the club king.

⁴ Responder's three-step response shows second-round club control.

⁵ Even if responder's club control is a singleton, there should be a good play for slam.

A jump shift rebid after a 1 ♣ opening bid and a positive notrump response is also an ace asking bid. In addition, Precision suggests that the jump shift response to an opening bid of 1 ◇, 1 ♡, or 1 ♠ may be treated as an ace asking bid.

When the opponents interfere

If the opponents attempt to jam your communications by overcalling an asking bid, strike back by changing your answer code:

Double = holding shown by a normal one-step reply;
Pass = holding shown by a normal two-step reply;
Bid one step above the overcall = holding shown by a normal three-step reply;
Bid two steps above the overcall = holding shown by a normal four-step reply;
And so on.

For example, if partner has just made a control asking bid of 4 ◇ and the next player tries to confuse the issue by over-calling with 4 ♠, respond as follows:

Double = no diamond control (the holding normally shown by a one-step answer to partner's control asking bid);
Pass = third-round diamond control (the holding normally shown by a two-step reply);
4 NT = second-round diamond control (a bid one step above the enemy overcall = holding shown by a normal three-step reply);
5 ♣ = first-round diamond control;
5 ◇ = first-round and second-round diamond control.

Similarly, if a trump asking bid is overcalled, a double shows a five-card suit missing all three top honors (the holding normally shown by a one-step answer), a pass shows a five-card suit headed by one of the top three honors (the holding normally shown by a two-step answer), a bid one step above the overcall shows a five-card suit headed by two of the top three honors, and so on.

A useful code name that will help you remember these methods may be obtained as follows:

> Double = 0 (worst possible holding)
> Pass = 1 (next worst possible holding)
> Code name = D0P1 or DOPI.*

If instead the opponents intervene with a double, no bidding room has been lost and the standard responses are retained.

---

* The name DOPI was first used to refer to one method for showing aces after an overcall of a Blackwood 4 NT bid (Double = 0 aces, Pass = 1 ace, bid one step above the overcall = 2 aces, and so on).

13

Defensive bidding

UNLESS YOU HAPPEN TO DISCOVER a method for repealing the law of averages, the opponents will at times strike first by making the opening bid. This chapter briefly summarizes the Precision recommendations for dealing with such unfortunate occurrences.

Defensive bidding after an opening bid of one of a suit

Simple suit overcalls

If your right-hand opponent opens the bidding with one of a suit, a simple suit overcall shows 11–15 high-card points and at least K Q 4 3 2 in the bid suit. Thus, it is very similar to a limited Precision opening bid. Let's look at some examples after a 1 ♡ opening bid by your right-hand opponent:

♠ K Q 7 6 3   ♡ J 8   ◇ A J 7 3   ♣ A 7:
Overcall 1 ♠.

♠ K Q J 10 7   ♡ 7 4 2   ◇ A 10 3   ♣ 6 2:
Overcall 1 ♠. You have only 10 high-card points, but the strong suit is sufficient compensation. The high-card point requirement for a simple suit overcall may be lowered slightly with a very good suit.

♠ 7   ♡ A 8 6   ◇ Q 8 5   ♣ A Q J 8 7 4:
Overcall 2 ♣.

♠ 7   ♡ A Q 4   ◊ K J 6 2   ♣ K 8 7 6 2:

Pass. Your club suit is not strong enough for an overcall.

Responses to simple suit overcalls are similar to the responses to the corresponding Precision limited opening bids.

Jump suit overcalls

A *jump* suit overcall of an opening bid of one of a suit shows a hand worth the corresponding preemptive opening bid (weak two-bid, three of a suit, or four of a suit). For example, bid as follows after a 1 ◊ opening bid on your right:

♠ A Q J 7 6 3   ♡ 7 2   ◊ 10 4   ♣ J 7 3:

Bid 2 ♠, showing a hand worth an opening weak two-bid in spades.

♠ 7   ♡ K Q J 9 7 6 3   ◊ Q 4 3   ♣ 6 2:

Bid 3 ♡ not vulnerable and 2 ♡ vulnerable, just as you would if you were opening the bidding.

♠ 4 3 2   ♡ —   ◊ 7 3   ♣ A Q J 10 8 7 4 2:

Bid 4 ♣ not vulnerable and 3 ♣ vulnerable.

♠ K Q J 10 7 6 3   ♡ A J 2   ◊ 4   ♣ K 2:

Bid 1 ♠. You have too much side-suit strength for a preempt.

♠ J 4 3   ♡ 7   ◊ 6 3 2   ♣ A Q J 9 7 4:

Pass. You are not strong enough for a simple 2 ♣ overcall or for a jump to the three-level.

Responses to jump suit overcalls are similar to the responses to the corresponding preemptive opening bids.

The 1 NT overcall

A 1 NT overcall shows the equivalent of a Goren 1 NT opening bid: 16–18 high-card points and balanced suit distribution. It also guarantees at least one stopper in the enemy suit. For example, if your right hand opponent opens with 1 ♠, overcall 1 NT with

♠ A J 7
♡ K Q 8 6
◊ A 9 7 6
♣ K 10

A 2 ♣ response by partner is non-forcing Stayman, any other new suit bid at the two-level is a signoff, notrump raises are natural, and a jump in a new suit below the game level is natural and forcing.

The takeout double

A double of an opening bid of one of a suit shows good support for all unbid suits and at least 13 high-card points. Partner is asked to bid his best suit. If he politely complies with this request but the takeout doubler corrects to a new suit of his own, the doubler is showing a good five-card or longer suit and 16 or more high-card points (i.e., a hand too strong for a simple overcall). If instead the takeout doubler rebids in notrump, he is showing at least one stopper in the enemy suit and 19 or more high-card points (i.e., a hand too strong for a 1 NT overcall). Some examples after an opening bid of 1 ◊ on your right:

♠ K Q 8 3   ♡ K Q 6 4   ◊ 7   ♣ K 10 7 3:
Double. You have 13 high-card points and excellent support for all unbid suits.

♠ A K 8 7 5   ♡ K J 7 4   ◊ 3   ♣ K 6 2:
Double. A 4–4 heart fit would be hard to find after 1 ♠ overcall.

♠ A K Q 8 6   ♡ 7 3   ◊ A K 6   ♣ J 6 3:
Double and bid spades next time. A 1 ♠ overcall would show a maximum of 15 points.

♠ K 8 3   ♡ K Q 6   ◇ A J 10 7   ♣ A Q 10:

Double and bid notrump next time. A 1 NT overcall would show a maximum of 18 points.

♠ 7 2   ♡ A 6 3 2   ◇ K 7 3   ♣ K Q J 4:

Pass. You cannot double with poor support for an unbid suit (especially an unbid major), and no other alternative is feasible.

The responses to a takeout double are very similar to those in standard Goren:

Simple new suit = 0–7 high-card points, usually a four-card or longer suit. (In some cases, it may be necessary to bid a three-card suit.)

Jump new suit = 8–10 high-card points, four-card or longer suit; not forcing. The high-card point requirement may be lowered slightly with a very strong suit or with a two-suited hand.

1 NT = 8–10 high-card points, at least one stopper in the enemy suit, and a balanced hand.

Cue-bid = 11 or more high-card points; forcing to game.

Pass = *Solid* five-card or longer holding in the enemy suit (K Q J 10 2 or better). Asks partner to lead a trump. (If your side doesn't draw trumps, the opponents will probably make their one-level contract by scoring a few top tricks and some ruffs.)

The cue-bid

In Precision, a cue-bid of the suit that the enemy has opened at the one-level shows a two-suited hand (5–5 distribution or better) and 14 or more high-card points. Partner is asked to choose his best unbid suit; if he picks the one that the cue-bidder doesn't have, the cue-bidder will let him know by repeating the cue-bid to ask for an alternate selection.

Jump NT overcalls

The Precision jump notrump overcall shows a minor two-suiter (5–5 distribution or better) and at least 11 high-card points. Partner is asked to bid his better minor.

Defensive bidding after a 1 NT opening bid

If the opponents open with a bid of 1 NT, Precision suggests the following procedures:

Double = balanced hand, same strength as that shown by the enemy 1 NT opening bid.

2 ♣ = minor two-suiter (5–5 distribution or better), 11 or more high-card points.

2 ♦ = major two-suiter (5–5 distribution or better), 11 or more high-card points.

A 2 ♥ or 2 ♠ overcall is natural and shows a very strong suit (usually six or more cards).

Defensive bidding after preemptive opening bids

Defensive bidding after a preemptive opening bid is a complex and controversial subject which is beyond the scope of this book. The following guidelines may prove helpful:

1] To overcall an enemy preempt, have a good opening bid with a very strong five-card or longer suit. With substantial extra strength, you may have to bid a mediocre suit, but avoid overcalling in weak suits. The bidding has been severely crowded by the preemptive opening bid, so your partner may have to pass or raise with inferior support; and the preempter's partner won't hesitate to make a devastating penalty double if he is looking at three or four trump tricks.

2] Double with 16 or more high-card points and no good suit to bid, and let partner decide what to do.*

---

* Alternatively, the Fishbein convention may be used: In second position, a double is for penalties, and an overcall in the next higher suit is conventional and forcing and asks partner to bid his best suit.

3] Don't let the preempt incite you into a foolhardy action; be prepared to concede an occasional loss to the opponents' preemptive tactics. When in doubt, pass and play safe. Not even experts always get to the best contract after such considerable interference!

14

Precision in the heat of battle

NOW THAT YOU HAVE LEARNED the Precision system, let's look at some of the hands that led to dramatic triumphs in championship play.*

1 ♣ opening bid: Deals 1, 7, 10, 11, 12, and 13.
1 ◇ opening bid: Deals 2 and 4.
1 ♡ or 1 ♠ opening bid: Deals 2, 6, and 9.
1 NT opening bid: Deal 3.
2 ♣ opening bid: Deal 9.
2 ◇ opening bid: Deals 5 and 8.
Asking bids: Deals 10 and 12.
The "impossible negative": Deal 13.

The 1969 world championships

A typical World Championship involves several months of intense competition. First, one six-man team is selected from each of four regions (Europe, the Far East, North America, and South America), usually by means of a series of grueling tournaments. Then, the four regional winners and the defending World Champions meet for the ten crucial days that will decide the bridge Champion of the World. A round-robin preliminary enables each of the five teams to face every opponent in head-to head competition; at the end of this stage, the two leading teams compete in a lengthy final match to determine the ultimate winner.

In the 1969 World Championships, hardly anyone was surprised when the great Italian Blue Team won its tenth World title; but virtually every bridge expert *was* amazed when a rela-

* Readers who wish to refer to hands illustrating specific aspects of the Precision system will find the following index helpful:

tively inexperienced Chinese team defeated far more practiced opponents from the United States, France, and Brazil and captured second place.* Here are some of the hands that helped forge this remarkable achievement.

DEAL 1

Dealer: E

Vulnerable: E-W

```
                    ♠ A J 9 7 4
                    ♡ A 7 6
                    ◊ A 6
                    ♣ A K 3
    ♠ 10 8 3              N          ♠ Q 6 5 2
    ♡ Q 10 8                         ♡ J 9 5 2
    ◊ Q 8 7         W         E      ◊ K 2
    ♣ 10 8 7 4             S         ♣ 9 6 2
                    ♠ K
                    ♡ K 4 3
                    ◊ J 10 9 5 4 3
                    ♣ Q J 5
```

The bidding:

SOUTH	WEST	NORTH	EAST
China	*U.S.*	*China*	*U.S.*
—	—	—	Pass
Pass	Pass	1 ♣	Pass
2 ◊	Pass	2 ♠	Pass
2 NT	Pass	3 NT	Pass
Pass	Pass		

Opening lead: ♡ 8

    In this hand from a round-robin match between China and the United States, China used the strong 1 ♣ opening bid to good advantage. After South's positive 2 ◊ response, North mentioned his spade suit; South bid 2 NT, showing a minimum positive response with poor spade support; and North proceeded directly to the best contract.

* Strictly speaking, the term "Chinese team" is somewhat of a misnomer. Two pairs were from Nationalist China (P. Huang and M. Tai; F. Huang and C. S. Shen), and one pair was from Thailand (K. W. Shen and Kovit Suchartkul). The non-playing Captain was C. C. Wei.

PRECISION SYSTEM

West led the heart eight, and declarer (C. S. Shen) ducked in both hands. Hearts were continued, and South won with the king and finessed the jack of diamonds. East captured this trick with his king and drove out the heart ace; but declarer simply cashed the diamond ace, entered his hand by leading a low club to the queen, and knocked out West's queen of diamonds, secure in the knowledge that the opponents could cash at most one more heart trick. When the thirteenth heart turned up in the East hand, declarer wound up with an overtrick.

When the United States held the North-South cards, the American North (using primarily standard methods) also thought it would be a fine idea to show his considerable strength immediately, and he opened the bidding with 2 NT. Unfortunately, this crowded the bidding so much that North and South didn't finish describing their hands (and exploring for slam) until the auction had reached the four-level, so North had to play the hand in *four* notrump. Under pressure because of the need to bring home ten tricks, he adopted a losing line of play; the contract was defeated by two tricks; and China scored a substantial gain of 11 IMPs.*

* Many bridge team tournaments, including the World Championships, are scored by International Match Points (IMPs). First, the score in each room is determined; on this hand, the Chinese North-South pair gained 430 points (130 trick score plus 300 points for making a non-vulnerable game) and the Chinese East-West pair gained 100 points (50 for each of the two undertricks), so the net gain for China was 530 points. Then, the net gain is converted to IMPs by using the following table:

Net Gain	IMPs	Net Gain	IMPs	Net Gain	IMPs
0–10	0	320–360	8	1300–1490	16
20–40	1	370–420	9	1500–1740	17
50–80	2	430–490	10	1750–1990	18
90–120	3	500–590	11	2000–2240	19
130–160	4	600–740	12	2250–2490	20
170–210	5	750–890	13	2500–2990	21
220–260	6	900–1090	14	3000–3490	22
270–310	7	1100–1290	15	3500–3990	23
				4000 and up	24

IMPs have the advantage of reducing the effects of major disasters. For example, a net loss of 3,000 points on one hand (which has hap-

In the next example, China scored a handsome gain by opening the bidding in both rooms.

DEAL 2

Dealer: W

Vulnerable: Both

```
                    ♠ 9 7 3
                    ♡ A Q 6 2
                    ◊ K Q 10 8 5
                    ♣ 6
      ♠ 6 5              N              ♠ A K Q
      ♡ K 8 5                           ♡ J 10 9 7 3
      ◊ J 4 3       W        E          ◊ 7 2
      ♣ Q 9 7 5 3       S              ♣ J 8 4
                    ♠ J 10 8 4 2
                    ♡ 4
                    ◊ A 9 6
                    ♣ A K 10 2
```

The bidding, Room A:

SOUTH	WEST	NORTH	EAST
China	*U.S.*	*China*	*U.S.*
—	Pass	1 ◊	1 ♡
1 ♠	Pass	1 NT	Pass
2 ♣	Pass	2 ♠	Pass
4 ♠	Pass	Pass	Pass

Opening lead: ♡ 5

The bidding, Room B:

SOUTH	WEST	NORTH	EAST
U.S.	*China*	*U.S.*	*China*
—	Pass	Pass	1 ♡
Double	2 ♡	2 NT	Pass
Pass	Pass		

Opening lead: ♠ A

pened, even to experts!) would almost surely mean the loss of the match if the scoring were by total points, and the remaining deals would become meaningless. A loss of 22 IMPs, although severe, can be recovered by several good results (such as a net gain of 500 points on each of two deals)

PRECISION SYSTEM

In Room A, the Chinese North confidently opened with a limited Precision 1 ◊ bid, and North-South had no trouble reaching the excellent spade game. Despite East's impressive trump holding, the defenders could win only three tricks; declarer (P. Huang) properly won the opening lead with the heart ace and played two rounds of trumps as soon as possible. Ultimately, declarer collected two spade tricks, one heart trick, five diamond tricks, and two club tricks for 620 points (120 trick score plus 500 for making a vulnerable game).

In Room B, the American North did not have the advantage of limited opening bids working for him and passed, fearing that an opening bid would promise a stronger hand and cause his partner to do something catastrophic. This enabled East to make a Precision opening bid of 1 ♡, thoroughly disrupting the Americans' normal channels of bidding. When the smoke had cleared, North and South discovered to their chagrin that they had missed a fine game contract, and North glumly took his nine tricks (two hearts, five diamonds, and two clubs) to net a mere 150 points (100 trick score plus 50 for making a part score). China thus registered a net gain on this deal of 470 points, or 10 IMPs.

The next deal illustrates two important advantages of the weak notrump: It immediately limits opener's hand, and the opponents often have great difficulty deciding how far to contest the auction.

DEAL 3   ♠ 4
Dealer: W   ♡ 5 4
Vulnerable: N-S   ◊ 8 6 5 4 2
        ♣ K J 9 8 7

  ♠ J 6 3 2   N   ♠ 10 9
  ♡ K 9 7 3   W   E   ♡ Q J 10 6 2
  ◊ A J   ◊ K 10 9 7
  ♣ A 5 2   S   ♣ Q 6

        ♠ A K Q 8 7 5
        ♡ A 8
        ◊ Q 3
        ♣ 10 4 3

The bidding, Room **A:**

SOUTH	WEST	NORTH	EAST
China	*U.S.*	*China*	*U.S.*
—	1 ♠	Pass	1 NT
Double	Pass	2 ♣	2 ♡
Pass	3 ♡	Pass	4 ♡
Pass	Pass	Pass	

    Opening lead: ♠ K

The bidding, Room **B:**

SOUTH	WEST	NORTH	EAST
U.S.	*China*	*U.S.*	*China*
—	1 NT	Pass	2 ♡
2 ♠	Pass	Pass	3 ◊
Pass	3 ♡	Pass	Pass
3 ♠	Double	Pass	Pass
Pass			

    Opening lead: ♡ 3

PRECISION SYSTEM

In Room A, the American West elected to open with an unlimited bid of 1 ♠, and his side didn't find out that game was hopelessly out of reach until after the dummy appeared. South cashed two spade tricks and shifted to a club, and the defenders easily registered a one-trick set.

In Room B, the limited 1 NT opening bid enabled the Chinese East to rule out game immediately, and he signed off in 2 ♡. South had considerable trouble determining the prospects for his side and competed once too often, and West made a lucrative penalty double. South grimly won the opening lead with the heart ace, cashed the three top trumps, and led a low club to dummy's jack. East won with the club queen and returned the ten of diamonds, and West topped South's queen with his ace. West then cashed the heart king and played another heart; South ruffed and played a club, won by West's ace. At this point, West committed a defensive faux pas; he cashed his high trump and played another heart, allowing South to ruff and discard his remaining losing diamond on one of dummy's good clubs. Nevertheless, the contract was down one (the defenders scored one spade, one heart, one diamond, and two clubs), and the 200-point profit meant a net gain for China of 250 points and 6 IMPs.

In our next deal, China confounded the U.S. team by opening with 1 ◊ in both rooms.

DEAL 4
Dealer: S
Vulnerable: E-W

```
                    ♠  10 8 6 5
                    ♡  10 6
                    ◇  A
                    ♣  A K 8 6 5 2
  ♠  K Q 4 2                         ♠  9 7
  ♡  A 9 7 2           N             ♡  Q J 5 4 3
  ◇  K Q 7 3       W       E         ◇  5 4 2
  ♣  9                 S             ♣  J 4 3
                    ♠  A J 3
                    ♡  K 8
                    ◇  J 10 9 8 6
                    ♣  Q 10 7
```

The bidding, Room A:

SOUTH	WEST	NORTH	EAST
China	*U.S.*	*China*	*U.S.*
1 ◇	Pass	2 ♣	Pass
3 ♣	Pass	3 ♠	Pass
3 NT	Pass	Pass	Pass

Opening lead: ♣ K

The bidding, Room B:

SOUTH	WEST	NORTH	EAST
U.S.	*China*	*U.S.*	*China*
Pass	1 ◇	2 ♣	Pass
2 NT	Pass	Pass	Pass

Opening lead: ♠ 2

PRECISION SYSTEM

In Room A, the Chinese South opened with a Precision 1 ◊ bid, and West had little choice but to pass. North and South proceeded to discover their club fit, shop around for a possible spade fit, and stop in 3 NT. This contract is a reasonable one in any case and cannot be defeated as the cards lie;* South (F. Huang) easily made an overtrick by capturing the spade king with his ace and returning the jack of spades, scoring three spade tricks, six club tricks, and one diamond trick —and 430 points.

In Room B, the American South didn't dare risk an unlimited opening bid, so West was able to open with 1 ◊. The Americans took over from that point, but could not reach game; South had to allow for the possibility of a modest overcall by North, and North never learned about the excellent club fit. The American declarer also managed to take ten tricks, but he scored only 180 points for his trouble; and China won 250 points and 6 IMPs.

In the finals, China found that when you are competing against the incomparable Italian Blue Team, superb bidding may well result in no better than a draw.

---

* A major-suit opening lead gives declarer his ninth trick. If instead West leads a low diamond, South wins in dummy, plays a small club to his queen, and leads the jack of diamonds. West wins, and has a most unhappy choice: He can surrender the crucial ninth trick by leading a major suit, or he can let declarer make an overtrick by setting up South's diamond suit. Finally, if West's opening lead is a club, South wins in his hand as cheaply as possible, plays a diamond to dummy's ace, enters his hand with a club, and plays a top diamond to present West with the same choice of disasters.

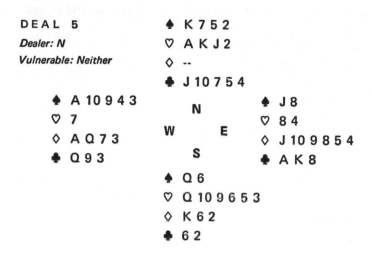

DEAL 5	♠ K 7 5 2
Dealer: N	♡ A K J 2
Vulnerable: Neither	◊ --
	♣ J 10 7 5 4

	♠ A 10 9 4 3			♠ J 8
	♡ 7		N	♡ 8 4
	◊ A Q 7 3	W	E	◊ J 10 9 8 5 4
	♣ Q 9 3		S	♣ A K 8

	♠ Q 6
	♡ Q 10 9 6 5 3
	◊ K 6 2
	♣ 6 2

The bidding:

SOUTH	WEST	NORTH	EAST
China	*Italy*	*China*	*Italy*
—	—	2 ◊	Pass
4 ♡	Pass	Pass	Pass

Opening lead: ♡ 7

The Chinese North opened with a Precision 2 ◊ bid,
showing 4-4-1-4 or 4-4-0-5 distribution with shortness in diamonds, and East had to pass. South (P. Huang) knew perfectly
well that game was a tossup in view of his modest strength, but
he also realized that terrible things might happen if the opponents were permitted to find their diamond fit. Therefore, he
jumped directly to 4 ♡; and East and West, who can make game
in diamonds by the simple expedient of taking the trump fi-
nesse, were completely shut out of the bidding. To make matters even worse for the Italians, declarer brought home his game
contract by setting up dummy's club suit for diamond discards,
and China collected 420 points.

Using standard bidding methods, North would open with
1 ♣, and East would overcall with 1 ◊ (or perhaps 2 ◊ if weak
jump overcalls are being used). Thereafter, East and West

would almost surely compete to the five-level and win the game bonus for themselves.

Unfortunately, the Italians don't use standard bidding methods either. The Italian North opened with 2 ♣; East feared to compete at the two-level with a jack-high suit and passed; and the Italians reached the heart game and made it. Thus, the precise Chinese bidding produced only a standoff— but that is no small achievement against the ten-time World Champions!

The 1970 world championships

In the 1970 World Championships, the Chinese team proved that the fine result of the previous year was no fluke. They captured second place once again, outperformed only by the powerful Dallas Aces.*

DEAL 6
Dealer: W
Vulnerable: N-S

```
                  ♠ J 10 3
                  ♡ 7 4 2
                  ◊ A Q 6 5
                  ♣ A 10 9
    ♠ 6 5                          ♠ A Q 9 7 4 2
    ♡ A Q 10 6       N             ♡ --
    ◊ 10 7 3     W       E         ◊ K J 4 2
    ♣ 7 5 4 2       S             ♣ K J 6
                  ♠ K 8
                  ♡ K J 9 8 5 3
                  ◊ 9 8
                  ♣ Q 8 3
```

* The 1970 Chinese team consisted of E. Hsiao and C. Cheng, P. Huang and M. Tai, and H. Lin; the non-playing Captain was D. Mao. The sixth Chinese player was unable to play due to ill health, which added considerably to the odds against the team in its quest for victory.

The bidding:

SOUTH	WEST	NORTH	EAST
U.S.	*China*	*U.S.*	*China*
—	Pass	Pass	1 ♠
Pass	Pass	1 NT	Pass
3 ♡	Pass	4 ♡	Pass
Pass	Double	Pass	Pass
Pass			

Opening lead: ♠ 6

In the above deal from a round-robin match between China and the Aces, the Chinese West (P. Huang) took advantage of the limited nature of his partner's 1 ♠ opening bid to lure his opponents into a deadly trap. After a standard opening bid of one of a suit, responder must bid with six or more points to prevent a missed game (and a furious partner). Playing Precision, Huang knew that East had at most 15 high-card points for his 1 ♠ bid and therefore passed with confidence. The Aces, keenly observing that the Chinese had abandoned the auction at the one-level, zoomed into game; whereupon Huang emerged with a devastating penalty double. Declarer could not avoid the obvious six losers—one spade, three trump tricks, one diamond, and one club—and the three-trick set gained 800 points for China.

In the other room, the Aces played in 3 ◊ with the East-West cards and were defeated by one trick. China thus scored an additional 50 points and registered a net gain for this deal of 850 points, or 13 IMPs.

Some bidding theorists argue that a conventional 1 ♣ opening bid is disadvantageous because opener does not show a good suit immediately. On the following deal from the round-robin, Italy* would have been much happier had they been playing against such theorists.

* *Not* the Blue Team, which had at long last retired to rest on its laurels

DEAL 7
Dealer: W
Vulnerable: E-W

```
                    ♠ 7
                    ♡ A Q 6
                    ◊ K J 10 5 2
                    ♣ K Q 10 4
    ♠ A Q J 10 8 4          N          ♠ --
    ♡ 7 5                              ♡ K 10 9 4
    ◊ A 6 4         W         E        ◊ Q 8 7 3
    ♣ A 2                   S          ♣ J 9 8 7 5
                    ♠ K 9 6 5 3 2
                    ♡ J 8 3 2
                    ◊ 9
                    ♣ 6 3
```

The bidding:

SOUTH	WEST	NORTH	EAST
Italy	*China*	*Italy*	*China*
—	1 ♣	1 ◊	2 ♣
2 ♠	Double	Pass	Pass
Pass			

Opening lead: ♣ A

The Chinese West properly promoted his 15-point hand because of the fine spade suit and opened with 1 ♣. North overcalled with 1 ◊, and East joined in by bidding 2 ♣ (recall that after an overcall, a Precision new suit bid shows 5–8 points and a five-card suit). South didn't want to be the only one to miss out on the action, so he competed with a bid of 2 ♠. West thought that he could defeat this contract, so he doubled.

West cheerfully cashed the club ace and shifted to a heart, and declarer tried to make the best of a very bad bargain by winning with dummy's ace and cashing the king and queen of clubs in order to discard his singleton diamond. West ruffed, however, and played a heart to East's king, and the jack of clubs return was ruffed low by declarer and overruffed by West. West then led the diamond ace; declarer ruffed and resignedly played a low spade, won by West's ten. West exited with a diamond and could not be prevented from making three more trump tricks, so China scored a three-trick set and 500 points.

In the other room, Italy played in 2 ♠ with the East-West cards and made it in spite of the terrible trump split. However, their reward was only 110 points, and China gained 390 points and 9 IMPs.

In the finals, China led at the end of the first quarter before succumbing to the superior might of the Dallas Aces. The following hand contributed to the Precision team's early lead.

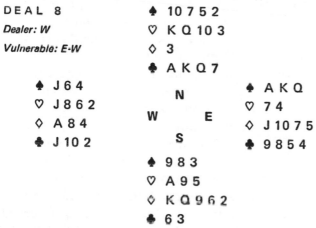

DEAL 8

Dealer: W

Vulnerable: E-W

```
                 ♠ 10 7 5 2
                 ♡ K Q 10 3
                 ◊ 3
                 ♣ A K Q 7
   ♠ J 6 4                      ♠ A K Q
   ♡ J 8 6 2        N           ♡ 7 4
   ◊ A 8 4       W     E        ◊ J 10 7 5
   ♣ J 10 2         S           ♣ 9 8 5 4
                 ♠ 9 8 3
                 ♡ A 9 5
                 ◊ K Q 9 6 2
                 ♣ 6 3
```

The bidding, Room A:

SOUTH	WEST	NORTH	EAST
China	*U.S.*	*China*	*U.S.*
—	Pass	2 ◊	Pass
2 ♡	Pass	Pass	Pass

Opening lead: ♡ 2

The bidding, Room B:

SOUTH	WEST	NORTH	EAST
U.S.	*China*	*U.S.*	*China*
—	Pass	1 ♣	Pass
1 ◊	Pass	1 ♡	Pass
2 ◊	Pass	Pass	Pass

Opening lead: ♣ J

PRECISION SYSTEM

The bidding, Room **B:**

SOUTH	WEST	NORTH	EAST
U.S.	*China*	*U.S.*	*China*
—	Pass	1 ♣	Pass
1 ◊	Pass	1 ♡	Pass
2 ◊	Pass	Pass	Pass

Opening lead: ♣ J

After the Chinese North in Room A opened with a highly descriptive Precision 2 ◊ bid, South quickly identified the best trump suit and signed off in 2 ♡. This contract proved to be ironclad despite South's limited supply of trumps; declarer knocked out the diamond ace and took one diamond trick, four heart tricks, two club tricks, and a club ruff to score 110 points.

In Room B, the American South faced a difficult decision at his second turn to bid and landed in an inferior contract. Declarer won the first trick in dummy and promptly cashed the rest of the top clubs in order to discard a losing spade. He then led a trump from dummy and guessed poorly by putting up his king; West, hoping to lead declarer astray, ducked smoothly. South now led a small trump, won by West's eight, and West shifted to a spade. East won and led the club nine; South elected to discard his last losing spade, and West also discarded a spade. East then led a high spade, which was ruffed by declarer.

South now tried to cash three top heart tricks, but East ruffed the third round with the ten of diamonds and returned his last spade to reach a crucial two-card end position. Declarer's last two cards were the Q 9 of diamonds, and he had to guess whether to ruff high or low. Misled by West's earlier duck in trumps, South went wrong and ruffed with the queen; West overruffed with the ace, and East captured the last trick with the diamond jack to register a one-trick set. Thus, China gained 160 points and 4 IMPs.

In our next example, the preemptive value of the Precision 2 ♣ opening bid resulted in a substantial gain for China.

DEAL 9
Dealer: E
Vulnerable: Both

```
                    ♠ K Q J 8 5
                    ♡ A
                    ◇ Q 8 4 3
                    ♣ K 3 2
     ♠ 10 6 4              N          ♠ 7 3 2
     ♡ J 9 8 7 4                      ♡ 6 2
     ◇ J 10 9 2      W         E      ◇ A K
     ♣ J                              ♣ A 10 8 7 6 4
                          S
                    ♠ A 9
                    ♡ K Q 10 5 3
                    ◇ J 8 5
                    ♣ Q 9 6
```

The bidding, Room A:

SOUTH	WEST	NORTH	EAST
China	*U.S.*	*China*	*U.S.*
—	—	—	Pass
1 ♡	Pass	1 ♠	2 ♣
Pass	Pass	2 ◇	Pass
2 NT	Pass	3 NT	Pass
Pass	Pass		

Opening lead: ♣ J

The bidding, Room B:

SOUTH	WEST	NORTH	EAST
U.S.	*China*	*U.S.*	*China*
—	—	—	2 ♣
Pass	Pass	2 ♠	Pass
Pass	Pass		

Opening lead: ◇ A

PRECISION SYSTEM

The American East in Room A chose to pass, whereupon North and South had no trouble reaching the best contract. The opening lead of the club jack was ducked by East and won by declarer's queen, and South cashed the heart and spade aces and ran all his heart and spade winners. With his contract safely home, he exited with a diamond; East won and had to yield an overtrick by leading into dummy's club king. China's score: 630 points.

In Room B, China struck the first blow by making the opening bid and enjoyed the last laugh with some devastating defense. After East's Precision 2 ♣ opening bid, the Aces never were able to determine that game was there for the taking. To add insult to injury, they couldn't even gain the lead until their modest spade partial had been defeated! East (H. Lin) cashed the two top diamonds and the club ace and led another club, West ruffed and returned a diamond, and East ruffed and gave West another club ruff to set the contract. China thus scored an additional 100 points and won 12 IMPs on this deal.

The 1970 U.S. Spingold team championship

In the 1970 U.S. Summer National Spingold Team Championship, a team of five young, lesser-known players used Precision to defeat America's top experts and win the coveted national title.* On the following hand, Precision asking bids avoided a disaster which the renowned opponents at the other table were unable to prevent.

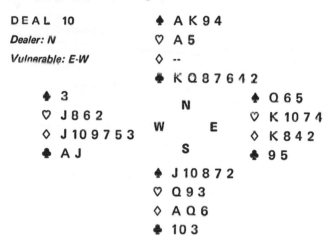

```
DEAL  10              ♠ A K 9 4
Dealer: N             ♡ A 5
Vulnerable: E-W       ◇ --
                      ♣ K Q 8 7 6 4 2
    ♠ 3                          ♠ Q 6 5
    ♡ J 8 6 2        N           ♡ K 10 7 4
    ◇ J 10 9 7 5 3  W     E      ◇ K 8 4 2
    ♣ A J            S           ♣ 9 5
                      ♠ J 10 8 7 2
                      ♡ Q 9 3
                      ◇ A Q 6
                      ♣ 10 3
```

The bidding:

SOUTH	WEST	NORTH	EAST
Smith		Weichsel	
—	—	1 ♣	Pass
1 ♠	Pass	2 ♠	Pass
2 NT	Pass	3 ♣	Pass
3 ♡	Pass	4 ♠	Pass
Pass	Pass		

Opening lead: ♣ A

---

* The team was captained by Steven Altman of New York City and included Thomas Smith of Greenwich, Conn., David Strasberg of Rockville Centre, N. Y., Joel Stuart of Forest Hills, N. Y., and Peter Weichsel of Rego Park, N. Y.

After North's 1 ♣ opening bid and South's positive 1 ♠ response, North (Peter Weichsel) put the trump asking bid into operation by raising to 2 ♠, and South's one-step 2 NT response showed a five-card spade suit missing all three top honors. North now made a control asking bid in clubs and found out that South had only third-round club control. Having determined (*below* the level of game!) that slam was a bad risk, North signed off in 4 ♠, and South made eleven tricks (and 450 points) when West led the ace of clubs and followed with the club jack.

Even a contract of 5 ♠ is in serious danger on this hand, as is evident from the unhappy fate that befell the highly esteemed pair of Alvin Roth and Tobias Stone in the other room. They bid all the way to 6 ♠, and West found the best opening lead —a heart. The defense therefore collected three tricks (one heart, one spade, and one club), and the Altman team gained 550 points and 11 IMPs.

In the finals, the Altman team defeated the Dallas Aces by 59 IMPs. The margin would have been even larger save for an uncharacteristic slip in declarer play by South on the following deal.

DEAL 11	♠ 6 3	
Dealer: S	♡ J 8 7 6	
Vulnerable: E-W	◊ 4 2	
	♣ A 9 8 7 2	

♠ A Q 7	**N**	♠ J 10 5
♡ Q		♡ 4 3 2
◊ A Q 9 7 5	**W** **E**	◊ J 10 8 6 3
♣ J 10 6 3	**S**	♣ Q 5

♠ K 9 8 4 2
♡ A K 10 9 5
◊ K
♣ K 4

The bidding, Room A:

SOUTH	WEST	NORTH	EAST
Strasberg		Altman	
1♣	Pass	1♢	Pass
1♠	Pass	2♣	Pass
2♡	Pass	4♡	Pass
Pass	Pass		

Opening lead: ♣3

The bidding, Room B:

SOUTH	WEST	NORTH	EAST
Aces		Aces	
1♠	Pass	Pass	Pass

Opening lead: ♣10

In Room A, Precision enabled North and South to reach the best contract. North's initial 1 ♢ response showed a maximum of 7 points, so he was not afraid to show his club suit at his second turn. South now had a chance to mention his heart suit, and North needed no further urging to contract for game.

In Room B, the wide range of South's unlimited 1 ♠ opening bid gave North an insoluble problem. He had to decide whether to bid with his minimal values and risk a catastrophic penalty if his partner were weak, or pass and risk missing a game if his partner were very strong. He elected to pass, and the Aces never discovered their heart fit.

The winning line of play in four hearts is to take the first trick with dummy's club ace and lead a spade to the king. West wins, and his best return is the ace and another diamond. South ruffs and concedes a spade, and the opponents force South to ruff another diamond. Declarer now cashes one high trump and ruffs a spade. The suit divides 3–3, compensating for the unfortunate location of the spade ace, so declarer draws trumps and claims his contract. Unfortunately, the Precision declarer selected a different plan and lost this particular battle; but he and his teammates went on to ultimate victory in the war for the national championship.

Other tournaments

Precision asking bids and careful declarer play combined to produce an impressive result on this hand from a 1970 French tournament.

DEAL 12

Dealer: E

Vulnerable: N-S

♠ 8 7 4	
♡ A K 8 5	
◇ A Q 10 6 3	
♣ A	

West		East
♠ 5 3	N	♠ A J 9 2
♡ J 3 2		♡ 4
◇ K J 4 2	W E	◇ 9 8 5
♣ 9 7 5 2	S	♣ Q J 6 4 3

♠ K Q 10 6	
♡ Q 10 9 7 6	
◇ 7	
♣ K 10 8	

The bidding:

SOUTH	WEST	NORTH	EAST
—	—	—	Pass
Pass	Pass	1 ♣	Pass
1 ♡	Pass	2 ♡	Pass
2 NT	Pass	3 ♠	Pass
4 ◇	Pass	5 ◇	Pass
5 ♠	Pass	6 ♡	Pass
Pass	Pass		

Opening lead: ♣ 2

North visualized slam as soon as he heard his partner's positive 1 ♡ response, and he began his exploration with a trump asking bid. South's two-step response showed five hearts to one of the top three honors and assured North that his side was unlikely to have any trump losers. North continued with a control asking bid in spades, and South's three-step answer showed second-round spade control.

Having ruled out the possibility of two fast spade losers, North now needed only to locate second-round diamond control to make slam a good bet, so he continued with a control asking bid of 5 ◊. North and South had agreed not to bypass the level of five of the agreed trump suit with only third-round control in the asked suit (that is, South would respond 5 ♡ with either no diamond control *or* third-round diamond control, 5 ♠ with second-round diamond control, and so on), so North was sure that he would reach slam only if South had the right hand—as, in fact, he did.

After winning the club lead in dummy, a good plan is to lead a spade immediately. East ducks, and South wins with the king. South now cashes the club king and discards a spade from dummy, ruffs a club, and plays dummy's last spade, forcing East to take his ace. Whatever East does now, South can ruff his losing spade in dummy, cash dummy's high hearts, return to his hand via a diamond ruff, and draw trumps. South did in fact make his slam and scored a sizable profit.

Our last example of the Precision system in the heat of battle is of American origin and was reported in the July 1970 issue of the *American Contract Bridge League Bulletin*. South reached an excellent contract but failed to find the winning line of play; can you do better?

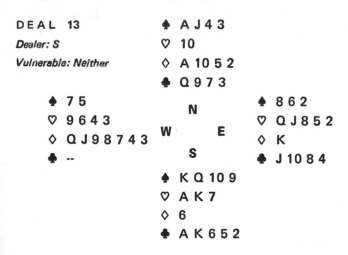

```
DEAL  13              ♠ A J 4 3
Dealer: S             ♡ 10
Vulnerable: Neither   ◊ A 10 5 2
                      ♣ Q 9 7 3
        ♠ 7 5                 N         ♠ 8 6 2
        ♡ 9 6 4 3                       ♡ Q J 8 5 2
        ◊ Q J 9 8 7 4 3   W       E     ◊ K
        ♣ --                 S         ♣ J 10 8 4
                      ♠ K Q 10 9
                      ♡ A K 7
                      ◊ 6
                      ♣ A K 6 5 2
```

PRECISION SYSTEM

The bidding:

SOUTH	WEST	NORTH	EAST
1 ♣	Pass	1 ◇	Pass
2 ♣	Pass	3 ♡	Pass
3 ♠	Pass	4 ♣	Pass
4 NT	Pass	5 ♡	Pass
7 ♠	Pass	Pass	Pass

Opening lead: ◇ Q

North jumped to 3 ♡ at his second turn to show an impossible negative with a singleton heart, and South bid 3 ♠ to designate the trump suit. When North bid 4 ♣, showing club support and extra values, South checked for aces via Blackwood and bid the grand slam in the 4–4 fit.

After winning the opening lead with dummy's diamond ace, the correct plan is to play just two rounds of trumps. When everyone follows suit, the contract will be laydown unless the clubs split 4–0, so play a high club *before* drawing the last trump. If everyone follows suit to this trick, simply extract the last trump and claim your contract. As the cards lie, West shows out but is unable to ruff; so you can cash two hearts and discard a club from dummy, ruff a heart, play two more rounds of clubs ending in your hand and ruff out that potentially fatal jack of clubs, reenter your hand with a diamond ruff, draw the last trump, and cash the good club to make your grand slam contract.

Appendix
The new frontiers
of Precision

THIS APPENDIX WILL OUTLINE some advanced procedures that may be of interest to experts and bidding theorists.

Auctions after a 1♣ opening bid
and interference above the level of 2♠

If partner opens the bidding with 1 ♣ and your right-hand opponent disrupts the auction by preempting at the level of 2 NT or higher, Precision suggests that your most important obligation is to inform partner about your controls so that he can determine slam prospects. As usual, an ace counts as 2 controls and a king is worth 1 control; in addition, a void *in the enemy suit* is worth 2 controls and a singleton in the enemy suit is worth 1 control. The following guidelines may prove helpful:

> Small slam normally requires 10 controls;
> Grand slam normally requires 12 controls;
> 1 ♣ opener normally has at least 5 controls.

Your possible responses are as follows:

1] Cue-bid of enemy suit = 4 or more controls with at least 1 control in the enemy suit; either good support for all unbid suits or a good long suit of your own. Opener should bid a five-card or longer suit if he has one. If not, he should either cue-bid the enemy suit to ask you to bid your best suit, or rebid in notrump if his strength is primarily in the enemy suit and he has a balanced hand. Game must be reached, and slam is probable.

2]   Bid 3 steps above the enemy overcall (*not* counting
     notrump in the steps) = 5 or more controls with *no* control
     in the enemy suit. Subsequent bidding is similar to that
     described above. Game must be reached, and slam is
     probable *if* opener can control the enemy suit.

3]   Bid 2 steps above the enemy overcall (*not* counting
     notrump in the steps) = 4 controls with *no* control in the
     enemy suit. Subsequent bidding is similar to that
     described above. Game must be reached, and slam is
     reasonably likely *if* opener can control the enemy suit.

4]   Bid 1 step above the enemy overcall (*not* counting
     notrump in the steps) = 3 controls. Game must be
     reached, and slam is possible if opener is markedly above
     minimum. Opener should cue-bid the enemy suit as a
     slam try with 7 or more controls.

5]   Bid 4 or more steps above the enemy overcall (*not*
     counting notrump in the steps) = natural, showing the
     equivalent of a Precision constructive response. Not
     forcing.

6]   Pass = Poor hand with no long suit and 0–2 controls;
     maximum of 7 high-card points. Opener's only forcing
     bids are (1) a double, which is for takeout, and (2) a
     cue-bid, which is forcing to game. A new-suit rebid by
     opener is natural and invitational to game.

7]   Double = For penalties. 4–7 high-card points, mostly in
     the enemy suit; 0–2 controls.

8]   3 NT = Balanced hand with at least one stopper in the
     enemy suit and 8–10 high-card points; 0–2 controls.

9]   4 NT = Blackwood. 4 or more controls; responder must
     be able to place the contract after hearing how many aces
     (and kings) opener has.

Rebids by 1♣ opener after a 2 NT response

A 2 NT response to a 1 ♣ opening bid shows either 11–13
high-card points or 16 or more high-card points. Precision has
developed the following rebid structure:

3 ♣ = modified Stayman. Responder answers as follows:

    3 ◊   = 11–13 high-card points, no four-card major, 4-4-3-2 distribution.

    3 ♡   = 11–13 high-card points, four-card heart suit. May have four-card spade suit.

    3 ♠   = 11–13 high-card points, four-card spade suit. No four-card heart suit.

    3 NT = 11–13 high-card points, no four-card major, 4-3-3-3 distribution.

    4 ♣   = 16 or more high-card points, four-card club suit. May have four-card diamond suit.

    4 ◊   = 16 or more high-card points, four-card diamond suit. No four-card club suit.

    4 ♡   = 16 or more high-card points, four-card heart suit. May have four-card spade suit.

    4 ♠   = 16 or more high-card points, four-card spade suit. No four-card heart suit.

3 ◊, **3** ♡, or **3**♠ = five-card or longer suit. Asks responder to raise with three-card or longer support.

Jump to **4** ♣ = Gerber ace-asking convention.

4 NT = Natural, invitational to 6 NT.

Rebids by 1 ♡ *or 1* ♠ *Opener After a 2 NT Response*

After a 1 ♡ or 1 ♠ opening bid and a 2 NT response, Precision has developed the following rebid structure:

Opener has weak balanced hand

    3 NT = 11–13 high-card points, balanced hand. Slam is remote, but responder may make a modified Stayman 4 ♣ bid with 19 or more high-card points.

Opener has weak unbalanced hand

    3 ♣   = 11–13 high-card points, unbalanced hand. Slam is unlikely. Responder may bid 3 ◊ to request

more information, and opener answers as follows:
New suit at three-level = four-card suit.
Rebid of major suit at three-level = six-card suit.
3 NT = five-card major suit and one or two four-card minor suits.
New suit at four-level = 5–5 two-suiter or better unsuitable for play in 3 NT.

Opener has strong balanced hand

4 NT = 14–15 high-card points, balanced hand; invitational to slam. Opener has one of the following three types of hands:
    a] 5-3-3-2 distribution with good five-card major suit missing at most one top honor (A or K or Q).
    b] 5-4-2-2 distribution with weak long suits and strong doubletons.
    c] 5-4-2-2 distribution with good four-card suit.
If responder wishes to know which of these hands opener has, he now bids 5 ♣. Opener rebids his major with type A, bids 5 NT with type B, and bids his four-card suit with type C.

Opener has strong unbalanced hand

The following rebids by opener show 14–15 high-card points and an unbalanced hand. Slam is very likely.

New suit at three-level = 5-4-3-1 or 5-4-4-0 distribution, four cards in bid suit.
Rebid of major suit at three-level = six-card major suit.
New suit at four-level = 5–5 two-suiter or better.
Rebid of major suit at four-level = *solid* six-card or longer major suit.

The texture asking bid

In addition to the asking bids presented in Chapter 12, Precision offers a *texture asking bid* which may be used in place of the control asking bid (i.e., after receiving an answer to a trump asking bid or ace asking bid). The answers are defined in terms of steps:

Steps Above Previous Bid	Holding in Asked Suit
1	No control, no support (xx or xxx)*
2	Control, no support (singleton or void)
3	Control, mild support (Ax or Kx)
4	No control, good support (xxxx or Qxx, or longer)
5	Control, good support (Kxx or Axx, or longer)
0	AQx or AKx, or longer
7	AKQ or longer

If the asking bidder wishes to receive further clarification, he makes another asking bid in the same suit that he just inquired about. Responder answers as follows:

Steps Above Previous Bid	Holding in Asked Suit
1	xx, x, Kx, xxx, Kxx, AQx
2	xxx, void, Ax, Qxx, Axx, AKx

Thus, the first step shows the poorer of the two possibilities shown by the response to the first asking bid, while the second step shows the better of the two possibilities.

If instead the asking bidder bids a new suit after receiving the answer to his first texture asking bid, he is making a new texture asking bid in the suit bid; any minimum bid in no-trump up to and including the level of 5 NT is Blackwood, asking for aces; and any rebid in the agreed-upon trump suit is a signoff.

* x = any small card.

Conventional 4♣ and 4♦ opening bids

Precision favors the use of a 4 ♣ opening bid to show 11–15 high-card points and a seven-card solid *heart* suit. A 4 ♡ response to this opening bid is a signoff, while a 4 ◊ response asks opener to cue-bid a side-suit ace or king if he has one and bid 4 ♡ if he does not. A 4 ◊ opening bid is similar except that opener's solid suit is in *spades*. Obviously, responder must never pass either of these opening bids!

The natural 1 NT response after a 1♣ opening bid and a one-level overcall

In Chapter 2, we saw that a 1 NT response after a 1 ♣ opening bid by partner and a one-level overcall by your right-hand opponent is forcing and shows an unbalanced hand with a good long suit. An alternative possibility, favored by some experts who have adopted the Precision system, is to use this 1 NT response as natural and not forcing, showing 8–10 high-card points and at least one stopper in the enemy suit. When using this treatment, a cue-bid of the enemy suit is used as the forcing bid with strong hands.

The intermediate 1♥ response to a 1♣ opening bid

Some experts have suggested using a 1 ♡ response to a 1 ♣ opening bid as conventional, showing 6–8 high-card points and any distribution. If responder has a true positive 1 ♡ response (8 or more high-card points and five or more hearts), he first bids 1 ♡ and then corrects his original message by bidding hearts again next time.

The strong 1♦ response

The most radical of the suggested modifications to the Precision system involves treating a 1 ◊ response to a 1 ♣ opening bid as the only *positive* response. The logic underlying this dramatic change is to provide as much bidding room as possible to probe for the best contract when both opener and responder have strong hands. It also permits responder to show his distribution quickly and naturally when his hand is weak. Here's how it works:

The 1 ♣ opening bid

1 ♣ opening bid = forcing, conventional. One of three types of hands:

    A. 18 or more high-card points, balanced hand.

    B. 16 or more high-card points, five-card or longer suit.

    C. 14 or more high-card points, distributional two-suiter with 7 or more playing tricks.

The first response

1 ◊ = positive, 8 or more high-card points. Forcing to game.

1 ♡ or 1 ♠ = 0–7 high-card points, four-card or longer suit. In some cases, it may be necessary to respond 1 ♡ with a short heart suit.

1 NT = 4–7 high-card points, no four-card or longer major suit, no five-card or longer minor suit.

2 NT = 8–10 high-card points largely in queens and jacks, no four-card or longer major suit, no *good* five-card or longer minor suit.

2 ♣ or 2 ◊ = 4–7 high-card points, good five-card or longer suit. No four-card or longer major suit.

2 ♡, 2 ♠, 3 ♣, 3 ◊, 3 ♡, or 3 ♠ = constructive response (the same as in standard Precision).

Opener's rebid after weak responses

Simple new suit = five-card or longer suit, not forcing. Responder makes a single raise with three-card or longer support and 0–4 high-card points and *jump* raises with three-card or longer support and 5–7 points.

Simple NT = 18–19 high-card points, balanced hand. Not forcing.

Jump to 2 NT = 20–21 high-card points, balanced hand. Not forcing.

Jump new suit = five-card or longer suit, one-round force. 22 or more high-card points or nine or more playing tricks with long suit.

Single raise of responder's suit = natural, not forcing. Responder should raise one more level with 5–7 high-card points (or with strong distributional values) and pass otherwise.

Opener's rebid after a positive 1 ◊ response

Simple new suit = five-card or longer suit. Responder makes a single raise with Jxx or better in support.

1 NT = 18–19 high-card points, balanced hand. A 2 ♣ rebid by responder is Stayman.

2 NT = 20–21 high-card points, balanced hand. A 3 ♣ rebid by responder is Stayman.

3 NT = 24–25 high-card points, balanced hand. A 4 ♣ rebid by responder is *modified* Stayman (asks for *any* four-card suit).

Jump new suit = ace asking bid. (See Chapter 12.)

A positive 1 ◊ response is forcing to game, so all of the above rebids are forcing (including 3 NT, after which slam is very probable).

Rebids by responder after a 1 ◊ positive response
and a suit rebid by opener

Single raise = 8 or more high-card points, at least three-card support, 0–3 controls. (Ace = 2 controls, king = 1 control.)

Jump raise = 11 or more high-card points, at least four-card support, 4 or more controls. Invitational to slam.

Simple NT = 8–10 high-card points, balanced hand, mild support (2–3 cards) for opener's suit.

Jump to 2 NT = 8 or more high-card points, 4-4-4-1 distribution with singleton in opener's suit.

3 NT = 14–15 high-card points, balanced hand, mild
support for opener's suit.

Simple new suit = 8 or more high-card points, five-card or
longer suit, poor support for opener's suit. A single
raise by opener is a trump asking bid (see Chapters
5, 12).

Jump new suit = 8 or more high-card points, 4-4-4-1
distribution, singleton in bid suit. Opener's next bid of
a suit fixes the trump suit.

*Rebids by responder after a 1 ◊ positive response
and a notrump rebid by opener*

Simple club bid = Stayman.

Simple new suit = five-card suit.

Jump new suit = 4-4-4-1 distribution, singleton in bid suit.

Jump to 4 ♣ = Gerber ace-asking convention.

4 NT = natural, invitational to 6 NT.

*Responses to a 1 ♣ opening bid after
an interfering double*

Pass = 0–3 high-card points.

Redouble = 8 or more high-card points. Equivalent to a
positive 1 ◊ response.

1 ◊ = 4–7 high-card points, at least one four-card and
one three-card major suit.

1 ♡ or 1 ♠ = 4–7 high-card points, five or more cards in
bid suit.

Other bids = same as if there were no interfering double.

Responses to 1 ♣ opening bid after an interfering overcall

Pass = 0–3 high-card points.

Double = negative; 4–7 high-card points with no five-card
or longer suit.

Simple new suit = 4–7 high-card points, five-card suit.

Jump new suit = 4–7 high-card points, six-card or
longer suit.

Simple NT = 8–10 high-card points, balanced hand, at
least one stopper in the enemy suit.

Cue-bid = 8 or more high-card points. Equivalent to a positive 1 ◊ response.

The 1 NT opening bid

So that a positive 1 ◊ response can be played as forcing to *game*, 1 ♣ is not opened with balanced hands unless you have at least 18 high-card points. This necessitates a change in the meaning of the 1 NT opening bid. One possibility is to use an opening bid of 1 NT to show 15–17 high-card points and a balanced hand, and open with 1 ◊ on any 13–14 point hand that would have qualified for a weak notrump opening bid in standard Precision.

Names _____ **Pair #** ____

General Approach __Simplified Precision__

	1♣	2♣	2-bids
Strong Forcing Opening	☒	☐	☐

SIMPLE OVERCALL
Normal Range __10__ to __15__ HCP

*Special resp. _____

SPECIAL DOUBLES
*Neg. Dbl. __Through 3◊__
_____

OPENING PREEMPTS
	Sound	Light	Solid Minor
3-bids	☒	☐	☐

NOTRUMP OVERCALLS
1 NT __16__ to __18__ HCP

Jump to 2 NT ____ to ____ HCP ☒ Unusual

*Other _____

PSYCHICS
Never	Rare	Occ.	Freq.
☐	☐	☐	☐

Describe: _____

JUMP OVERCALL
Strong ☐ Interm. ☐ Preempt ☒

OVER OPP'S TAKEOUT DBL.
New suit ☐ Nonforc. ☒ Forc.

	Forc.	Good	Weak
Jump shift	☐	☒	☐

*Other __2NT a raise__

OVER OPP'S PREEMPTS
	Takeout	Opt.	Penalty
Dbl. is	☐	☒	☐

*Conv. takeout _____

OVER OPP'S 1 NT OPENING
☒ 2♣ __for minors__

*Other __2◊ for majors__
_____

DIRECT CUE-BIDS
☒ Strong T/O ☐ Natural _____

OTHER CONVENTIONAL CALLS
• _____
_____

SLAM CONVENTIONS
☐ Gerber: _____ ☒ 4 NT Var.: __Blackwood__

*Other __DOPI__

DEFENSIVE CARD PLAY
From three small, tend to lead ☐ high ☐ middle ☐ low

*MUST ALERT

NOTRUMP OPENING BIDS
1 NT __13__ to __15__ HCP   2 NT __22__ to __24__ HCP

3 NT ____ to ____ HCP

STAYMAN
2♣ ☐ Forc. ☒ Nonforc.   ☒ Solid Suit: __Minor__

2◊ ☒ Forc. ☐ Nonforc.   _____

*Other __Stayman after NT responses to 1♣__
opening

MAJOR OPENINGS
1♡–1♠ opening on 4 cards

	Often	Seldom	Never
1st-2nd	☐	☒	☐
3rd-4th	☐	☒	☐

MINOR OPENINGS
Length promised

	4+	3+	Shorter
1♣	☐	☐	☒
1◊	☐	☒	• ____

RESPONSES
Jump Raise ☐ Forc. ☒ Limit

*Other __1 NT, 2NT forcing__

RESPONSES
Jump Raise ☐ Forc. ☒ Limit

*1 ◊ resp. __0-7 HCP, negative__

• Other __Inverted ◊__

OPENING TWO-BIDS
(circle where applicable) "2♣ STRONG" only artificial bid allowed

2♣ ②◊ WEAK __6__ to __10__ HCP: __Good suit__

②♡ ②♠ Forc. resp. ☒ new suit ☒ 2 NT

②♣ 2◊ INTERM. __11__ to __15__ HCP: __Good suit__
2♡ 2♠ ☐ 2 NT Negative

2♣ 2◊ STRONG ____ to ____ HCP: _____
2♡ 2♠ ☐ 2 NT Negative

* MUST ALERT